Strictly
Speaking

Strictly Speaking

WILL AMERICA BE THE DEATH OF ENGLISH?

EDWIN NEWMAN

G.K.HALL & CO.

 Boston, Massachusetts

1975

Library of Congress Cataloging in Publication Data

Newman, Edwin.
  Strictly speaking.

  Large print ed.
  1.   English language in the United States.
  2.   Sociolinguistics.   3.   United States — Social life
  and customs.   4.   Sight-saving books.   I.   Title.
  PE2808.N4 1975   301.2'1   74-9827
  ISBN 0-8161-6297-2

Published in Large Print by arrangement with The Bobbs-Merrill Company, Inc.

Set in Photon 18 pt Crown

Portions of this book have appeared in slightly different form in the *Atlantic Monthly,* Overseas Press Club *Bulletin, Punch,* and TV *Guide.*

Grateful acknowledgment is made for permission to use the following:

Excerpts from "Cocktails for Two" by Arthur Johnston and Sam Coslow, copyright © 1934 by Famous Music Corporation. Copyright renewed 1961 by Famous Music Corporation.

Excerpts from "The Birth of the Blues" by B. G. DeSylva, Lew Brown and Ray Henderson, copyright © 1926 by Harms, Inc. Copyright renewed. All rights reserved. Used by permission of Warner Bros. Music.

For
my wife
and
daughter

CONTENTS

ACKNOWLEDGMENTS

This book is dedicated to my wife and daughter. My wife's contributions have been so many and varied that it is not possible to list them. There would be no book without her. My daughter supplied many suggestions, much encouragement, and, through the years, tolerance of my kind of humor above and beyond the call of duty.

Jeannette Hopkins provided the impetus for the book and edited it. Carol Bok did the typing and the research. To both of them, my deep thanks. Mary Heathcote was the invaluable copy editor.

I want also to thank NBC News, on whose time and in whose employ I had many of the experiences and gathered much of the material on which the book is based. The NBC library gave generous help.

Finally, for permission to use, mostly in changed form, material that originally appeared in their pages, I thank the *Atlantic Monthly, TV Guide,* Overseas Press Club *Bulletin,* and *Punch.*

Strictly
Speaking

INTRODUCTION:

A Protective Interest in the English Language

Will America be the death of English? I'm glad I asked me that. My well-thought-out mature judgment is that it will. The outlook is dire; it is a later point in time than you think. The evidence is all around us:

In March, 1974, the White House press secretary, Ron Ziegler, explained a request for a four-day extension of a subpoena from the Watergate prosecutor for certain files. The extension was needed, Ziegler said, so that James St. Clair, President Nixon's attorney, could "evaluate and make a judgment in terms of a response."

We are all of us ready to man the barricades for the right to evaluate and make a judgment in terms of a response, but Ziegler could have said that St. Clair wanted more time to think about it. That he didn't is a commentary on the state of language in the United States, and the state of the language is a commentary on the state of our society. It must be obvious that our society, like our language, is in serious trouble when a man who represents the President speaks of evaluating and making a judgment in terms of a response; when the President himself feels no embarrassment (on any score, apparently) in saying, "There must be no whitewash at the White House," describes a possible course of action as taking the hang-out road, and, on asking his legal counsel for a detailed statement, is told, "Let me give you my overall first"; when a vice-president of the United States achieves fame of a sort through alliterative device: "pampered prodigies," "vicars of vacillation," "nattering nabobs of negativism"; when his successor denounces "prophets of

2

negativity'' and endorses the administration ''policy-wise''; when Mayor John Lindsay of New York, about to step down, says that his youngest child will go to a boys' school because ''he needs peer stuff''; when a publisher will put out what purports to be a book of poetry, *Pages,* by Aram Saroyan, in which, occupying an entire page, this constitutes a poem: ''Something moving in the garden a cat''; and this: ''incomprehensible birds''; and this: ''Alice''; and this: ''lobstee''; and when nobody takes medicine but rather medication. Indian tribes soon will have medication men. Ours is a time when Secretary of the Treasury William Simon advises Congress, ''One cannot ad hoc tax reform.'' He might have added that there are no bargains at ad hoc shops.

It is a time when, in the interest of fuel conservation, the federal government adopted the comic strip character Snoopy as a symbol and showed us Snoopy on top of his dog house, flat on his back, with a balloon coming out of his mouth containing the words, ''I believe in conserving energy!'' while below there was this exhortation: savEnergy

savEnergy. An entire letter e at the end of save was savd. In addition, an entire space was savd. Perhaps the government should say onlYou can prevent forest fires.

Ours is also a time when Harry Ashmore, a former newspaper editor apparently overborne by being president of the Center for the Study of Democratic Insititutions, describes an idea he considers unfounded as ''a spurious construct,'' and speaks of television in a presidential election year as facing ''the quadrennial challenge of giving focus and perspective to the polemics of contending partisans''; and when one of Ashmore's associates, a writer, gives his occupation as social critic. (''What do you want to be when you grow up, son?'' ''Gee, Dad, I thought I'd be a social critic.'') And when the president of the Organization of American Historians, John Hope Franklin, identifies 1974 as ''this antepenultimate year of our bicentennial.''

There are those who think it better to say impacted on than hit. A young actress said she hoped she would not be made an escapegoat if the show she was in failed. An author told me there was too much largis available in Washington. Derbis, the stuff that lies around after a wreck, is part of history at NBC News. So is a letter from a viewer who thought she saw — I don't remember in what connection — the hammer and cycle on one of our programs, possibly a program on which another viewer accused us of providing grist for the fires. Hubert Humphrey has said more than once that he believes in going at politics hook and tong. Others of strong ambition believe, perhaps, in going at it hook and ladder.

I have seen scripts by television news writers who proposed to tell the American people that "Old Man Winter wound up today and threw a roundhouse punch." Ron Ziegler (Again? Yes. After all, spokesmen are made to be quoted) believes that a photograph of someone taken with the President might be sent to that person as a momento. A guest on the

"Today" show assured me that blacks running rampart through the streets were not representative of most blacks in this country. Kevin White, mayor of Boston, has spoken of "young juveniles." Dr. Oscar Sussman of the New Jersey State Health Department wondered aloud during a television interview: "Can we stop something, preventive medicinewise, from happening?" There are people who speak of seven A.M. in the morning and four P.M. in the afternoon; I heard that on the NBC television station in Los Angeles. On the ABC station in Washington, a newscaster spoke of three families that had suffered kidnapings as having the same thing in common.

Most conversation these days is as pleasing to the ear as a Flash-Frozen Wonder Dinner is to the palate, consisting largely of "You've got to be kidding," "It's a bad scene," "How does that grab you?" "Just for openers," "It's a fun idea," "Fantastic," "It's the in place," "Is he for real?" "Back to square one," "I just heard this great Polish [Hungarian, Italian, etc.] joke," "That's the name of the game," "Who's counting?" "That's the bottom line," "Wild," "What's the plot?" "Would you believe?" "Out of sight," "Lots of luck," "What can I tell you?" "What have you done for me lately?" and "How do you structure your day?"*

There is a recording of Sammy Davis, Jr., singing "And then they nursed it, rehearsed it, And gave out the news — You better believe it — That the Southland gave birth to the blues." Inserting "You better believe it" must have seemed a fun idea at the time. In the same way, wearing a button with somebody else's commercially produced clever remark on it or the apron bearing the words "For this I spent four years in college?" seems to many great for

---

* Also "I feel so vulnerable," I feel threatened," Will the real _____ please stand up?" "Back to the drawing board," "I've got news for you," "I couldn't care less," "Meanwhile, back at the ranch," "What is your philosophy on that?" "Let me give you my thinking on that," "Can do," "No can do," "The _____ bit," "Track record," "For the birds," "He's inner-directed but she's outer-directed."

openers, even to many who spent four years in college. The conversation thus opened, "Everything you ever wanted to know about . . . but were afraid to ask," and ". . . is alive and well and living in . . ." soon make it a new ball game.

Language is in decline. Not only has eloquence departed but simple, direct speech as well, though pomposity and banality have not. Some who share my views on this believe that one of the nation's most pressing needs is an Anti-Thrust Act. ("What is the thrust of your report?") Others believe that if there is one word that expresses the spirit of the age, it is parameter, a mathematical term now widely misused so that nobody finds himself in the hateful position of having to say boundary or limit. I would choose viable. Thus Senator Howard Baker, Republican of Tennessee, commenting on Judge John Sirica's decision to give the Watergate grand jury's report on President Nixon to the House Judiciary Committee, was not content to say that the judge had no alternative. He said that Sirica had no viable alternative.

I don't know what Baker thought it added, but automatic recall should be visited on anyone on the public payroll who says viable. Something drastic is needed, for while language — the poor state of language in the United States — may not be at the heart of our problems, it isn't divorced from them either. It is at least conceivable that our politics would be improved if our English were, and so would other parts of our national life. If we were more careful about what we say, and how, we might be more critical and less gullible. Those for whom words have lost their value are likely to find that ideas have also lost their value. Maybe some people discipline themselves in one and not in the other, but they must be rare.

Jack Gould, when he was television critic of the *New York Times,* thought a sticky wicket was something you squeezed through. Howard Cosell noted that the result of a particular athletic event left the French people "numbstruck." I regret that I do not remember how this, to use one of Cosell's favorite words, eventuated. An official of the office of Economic Opportunity was quoted as saying, "That's the loggerhead no one has yet gotten past." There is an apartment building in Miami Beach known as the Maison Grandé. There was a massage parlor in New York called the Club Monmarté. I have eaten Béaucoup Mints. In Wilkes-Barre, Pennsylvania, you may purchase a Monseur hairpiece. At the Ramada Inn in Washington, D.C., you will find the Haypenny Bar.

Is it important? Obviously much of it isn't. The drinks at the Haypenny Bar probably would be no better or worse if the spelling were more nearly authentic, and the Béaucoup Mints would not have had a mintier taste without the uncalled-for acute accent, which, by the way, was the accent that appeared over the last letter in the name of W. C. Fields's alter ego, Egbert Sousé. Fields, probably because he liked the sound in French, always referred to it as an accent grave.

A world without mistakes would unquestionably be less fun. I cherish the memory of the Long Island Railroad union leader who felt he was chasing Willie the Wisp during contract negotiations, and I thank the *New York Post* for describing Ho Chi Minh as a small wisp of a man, for it thereby left no stone unturned and no stone not turned over as well. Nor will I ever forget the estate agent in Norwich, England, who told us that we should not expect that city to be like the metrolopis. A friend of my early youth thought that the English actor Clive Brook was Civil Brook, and my life has been richer for it. What could be more civil than a brook? And I have only the kindest memories of a colleague in the navy in World War II who wanted to know what a lert was, inasmuch as we were about to go on one.

There is a story, which I am assured is true, about the caretaker of a cemetery in Barbados that had a particularly interesting tomb. One day a number of women came to see it without making arrangements beforehand. The caretaker felt they were presuming and wanted to be certain that his gesture was not misunderstood. "I'll show it to you ladies," he said, "but don't get the idea that I am going to be here to show it to Bobtail and his crew." How can language be better served than that?

How can it be served better than it was by the taxi driver who told me how much he admired the actress Mildred Natwick? "Ah," he said, nodding, "she can portray."

Harry Truman used to say irrevelant and stress the third syllable in incomparable. But Mr. Truman never had any trouble getting his points across.

As a veteran I was in an army hospital in 1947, and a fellow patient asked me what another patient did for a living. I said he was a teacher. "Oh," was the reply, "them is my chief dread." A lifetime was summed up in those six syllables. There is no way to improve on that.

In 1950 two members of the British Foreign Office, Guy Burgess and Donald Maclean, defected to the Russians and became notorious as "The Missing Diplomats." On the trail too late, like dozens of other reporters, I went to Maclean's house in Buckinghamshire and found only the gardener on the premises. I asked what his reaction had been on hearing the news. He was a country man. "Oi were thunderstruck," he said.

There is no way to improve on that, either.

The argument for preciseness of language has limits, of course. I don't know whether grammarians were less taken in by, for example, the Gulf of Tonkin affair than other groups in the population. I assume that professors of logic often arrive at the wrong conclusion. Nine justices of the United States Supreme Court may consult the same laws, check the same precedents, and come out with contradictory conclusions, elegantly expressed. Certainly, too, those involved in Watergate had had far more education than the national average. Yet one of the things the Watergate hearings revealed was a poverty of expression, an inability to say anything in a striking way, an addiction to a language that was almost denatured, and in which what little humor did occur was usually unintentional.

It has often been said that the Watergate people hid what they were doing from themselves behind a cloud of fuzzy notions they never rigorously examined. I am more inclined to believe that they knew what they were doing and did it, for the most part, out of plain self-interest. But the fuzzy notions provided an easy escape. The haven was there, for those who wanted it, in phrases like "higher national interest," "excess of zeal" (looked at this way, the Nixon administration's major problem was zeal production's outrunning the demand for it), "good team player," and the like.

Watergate, in the course of revealing so much else about American life, also revealed the sad state of language; apparently form and substance are related. In Washington, as we learned from the White House transcripts, a president may speak of kicking butts, call a problem a can of worms, decide not to be in the position of basically hunkering down, anticipate something hitting the fan, propose to tough it through, sight minefields down the road, see somebody playing hard ball, claim political savvy, and wonder what stroke some of his associates have with others. He may be told by members of his staff what is the bottom line, that a situation has cycled somewhat while another situation is a bullet biter, that a lawyer has done some dove-tailing for him, that a lot of people have to pull oars, and that another man was a ballplayer who carried tremendous water for the President's cause. That was private talk; in public, Watergate language lost the men's club flavor and became distended. In addition to the notorious "at that point in time," first cousin to "in point of fact," John Ehrlichman spoke of "that time era," and John Mitchell of "that time frame," though Ehrlichman did say "labor the point" rather than "belabor the point," a heroic act in the circumstances.

In Watergate, nobody ever discussed a subject. It was always subject matter. The discussion never took place before a particular date. It was always prior to.

Nor was anything said, it was indicated; just as nothing was done, it was undertaken. If it was undertaken, it was never after the indications about the subject matter; it was subsequent to them. A danger in using subsequent is that some people think it means before rather than after, which made the Watergate hearings, to which subsequent was almost a password, even harder to follow. Those hearings popped up, ghostlike, at the trial in New York of John Mitchell and Maurice Stans, during the cross-examination of John Dean:

PROSECUTOR: Am I correct that you approached various prosecutors and asked for immunity from prosecution in return for your testimony?

DEAN: No, sir.

PROSECUTOR: Did your lawyer do it?

DEAN: Yes, sir.

PROSECUTOR: You haven't taken the Fifth Amendment before another grand jury?

DEAN: Subsequent to my appearance here, yes.

Ah, Watergate! John Mitchell, former

attorney general of the United States, spoke of "grievious" damage and "dilatorious" action. Sam Ervin, senator from North Carolina and chairman of the Watergate Committee, thought claims should be "substantuated" and discerned "gradiations" of difference. A White House lawyer, Richard Moore, spoke, as he put it, "in the context of hindsight." Herbert Kalmbach, President Nixon's personal attorney or not President Nixon's personal attorney, as the case may be, while telling the Senate committee of his changing "level of concern," referred to "the meeting I recall with particularity."

Language used to obfuscate or conceal or dress with false dignity is not confined to politics and did not burst upon us for the first time with Watergate. In our time, however, it has achieved a greater acceptance than ever before, so that stiffness and bloat are almost everywhere. Any number of people might render the line in the television commercial, "I ate the whole thing," as "I ate the thing in its totality." In Britain, this sign was chalked on the blackboard at London Airport: "All BEA flights subject to delays, reactionary to fog at Heathrow Airport earlier this morning." My daughter spotted a sign that urged restaurant employes in an English city to use "any hygienic hand washing media." But while this has been going on in part of our society, a different process has been under way in another part, where respect for rules has been breaking down and correct expression is considered almost a badge of dishonor.

I believe that the decline in language stems in part from large causes. One of those causes is the great and rapid change this country went through in the 1960s. Take the environment issue. It raised questions that challenged the fundamental assumptions of American life. Is it sensible to consume as much as we do? How do you calculate a standard of living — do you include quality of air and water, for example, and the amount of time you spend in traffic jams? Is economic growth necessarily a good thing? What social obligations does a corporation take on when it builds a plant to earn profits?

Another aspect of that change was that people who felt oppressed by society organized to enforce their demands either for the first time or with greater success than ever before — blacks, Indians, Chicanos, women, homosexuals, lesbians, prison inmates, welfare recipients. Perhaps the most remarkable manifestation of this was the strike by black garbage collectors in Memphis, Tennessee, during which Martin Luther King, Jr., was killed. A few years earlier such a strike would have been unimaginable.

It came as a shock that all these groups could bargain with society over what they wanted, and that made older and more settled people uncomfortable. But the greatest capacity for creating such discomfort lay with those things that reminded people of their age, reminded them that the future did not belong to them and that maybe not even the present did. Thus the generation gap.

Here I must pause to say that the

generation gap is not something I fully accept. Still less is it something I unreservedly deplore. The notion that the trouble between generations is caused by a failure in communication may have some merit, but it makes a large and not necessarily justified assumption: that there should be communication and that if there is, things will be better. I am not so sure. It may be that we have entered a time when some groups would do better to ignore each other than to communicate with each other. Not communicating saves energy; it keeps people from worrying about things they cannot do anything about; and it eliminates an enormous amount of useless talk.

I take myself as an example. I have no wish to dress as many younger people do nowadays. I cannot accept the discomfort that many of them do, or the lack of privacy. I have no wish to impair my hearing by listening to their music, and a communication gap between an electronic rock group and me is something I devotedly cherish and would hate to see disappear.

Or take the job of drama critic, which I happened to have at NBC in New York for six seasons, 1965 - 66 through 1970 - 71. It was often troublesome and annoying, not because most of the plays were bad, although they were. It was because a number of the plays I saw did not seem to be directed at me, but at younger people.

I watched these plays and, it sometimes happened, I got little out of them. Inevitably I asked myself whether there was something wrong with me. For example, in the 1968 - 69 season there was a play called *Beclch,* which, if you examine it, is "Belch" with an extra c in it.

The character of that name was a white queen somewhere in Africa, where she ruled in an amorous, bloodthirsty, and extremely verbose way. The action of the play included shouting, scratching, fighting, lovemaking, biting, dancing, massage, murder, fits, ritual slaughter, nudity, and self-strangulation. The climax of the play came when one of the male characters, who was naked apart from elephantiasis makeup on one leg, choked himself to death. It took him quite a long time, and all I learned from the scene was that he had red hair, and I wondered whether the lack was in me.

This was not a matter of great importance in itself. Nonetheless, *Beclch* did symbolize the difficulties that come with age, when change is taking place and you are not among those changing. For *Beclch* was a product of the cult of youth and the cult of change, cults in whose creation the war in Vietnam played an enormous part. Because people of age and experience and position led us into Vietnam, they made age and experience and position look ridiculous. This conferred a kind of blessing on youth and inexperience and not being in the establishment. To many it made change and experiment intrinsically desirable. The effect was almost beyond measuring, and we still do not know its full extent, but we do know that when age, experience, and position were discredited, there was a wholesale breakdown in the enforcement of rules, and in the rules of language more than most. One reason is that, in language, changes can be registered quickly and passed along literally by word of mouth. Another reason is that the language people use is a ready guide to the side they are on, and correct and relatively conventional language was widely abandoned by those in revolt. Finally, language lies to hand not only as a symbol of change but as its instrument.

Television played its part, too. It exalted the picture and depreciated the word. The "talking head" — which may someday take its place as a name for English pubs alongside the King's Heads and Boar's Heads and Saracen's Heads and the rest — was considered dull television and to be avoided whenever possible in favor of something, anything, moving, though a head that talks well is a pearl beyond price.

The decline in language comes in part, as I said, from such large causes. It also stems from the naïve but stuffy conviction that certain occasions call ineluctably for an idiom that is, somehow, worthy. In June, 1972, I recall, the unwelcome news came that the government of the state of Connecticut, which had been looking for a state song for six months, had found one. As could easily have been predicted, the song is terrible. Maybe the music isn't; I have not heard it. But the words are. What is worse, the new song means that the Yale University fight song, "Boola Boola," which had sneaked in in the absence of an official song, will no longer be played on official occasions in Connecticut.

It was Governor Thomas Meskill who recommended that the state legislature adopt "The Hills of Connecticut" as the official song. This is how it goes:

> There's a place that's nearest to
>   heaven,
> Where the hills roll up to the sky,
> And the land is peaceful and lovely,
> It's where I want to live and die.
> I love the hills of Connecticut,
> I love its valleys and its streams,
> I've got my loved ones in
>   Connecticut,
> And they're always in my dreams.
> My heart is home among those

friendly hills,
And no matter where I roam,
I love the hills of my Connecticut,
Connecticut, my home.

Those are unexceptionable sentiments, but we have thousands of songs about valleys and streams, and people in our dreams, and no matter where we roam, and this and that, my home. Compare those sentiments with what they replaced:

"Boola boola, boola boola, boola boola, boola boola, boola boola, boola boola, boola boola, boola boo."

I checked with Yale University and found that there are additional words — the usual stuff about what the Yales intend to do to the Harvards and the Princetons on the fields of friendly strife. I also learned that boola boola is an adaptation of the Hawaiian hoola boola, which is a term of exultation and ecstasy used to accent the rhythm of dances. But those are irrelevancies. For the last seven decades, when the Yales have sung Boola boola, boola boola, boola boola, boola

boola, boola boola, boola boola, boola boola, boola boo, that simple affirmative statement is all they had in mind.

In 1972, the same year that gave the world "The Hills of Connecticut," Gough Whitlam became prime minister of Australia on a platform that included the promise of a new national anthem to replace "God Save the Queen." The winner, established by public opinion poll, was "Advance Australia Fair," a song that already existed. The Australian government takes the position that only the music matters; the words that go with the tune are not regarded as part of the official anthem. One would like to think that its view has something to do with what the words, written by P. D. McCormick in 1885, are, but that is unlikely.

In any case, the lyrics *are* sung, and have drawn a complaint from the Women's Electoral Lobby, though on feminist rather than literary grounds. There are four stanzas; here are one and three:

Australia's sons, let us rejoice,
For we are young and free;
We've golden soil and wealth for toil,
Our home is girt by sea;
Our land abounds in nature's gifts
Of beauty rich and rare;
In history's page, let every stage
Advance Australia fair.
In joyful strains then let us sing
Advance Australia fair.

While other nations of the globe
Behold us from afar,
We'll rise to high renown
And shine like our glorious southern
   star.
From England, Scotia, Erin's Isle,
Who come our lot to share
Let all combine with heart and
   hand to
Advance Australia fair.

Connecticut also abounds in gifts of
beauty rich and rare, though "The Hills of
Connecticut" is conspicuously not among
them. Governor Meskill, on hearing of my
objections to the song, remarked that I

27

had a nose for news but no ear for music. A good line for a governor, better than we expect. But when the Governor announced that he would not run for reelection in 1974, I was not sad. He has done enough. Can a state song be repealed?

Can a *phrase* be repealed? I have in mind Y'know. The prevalence of Y'know is one of the most far-reaching and depressing developments of our time, disfiguring conversation wherever you go. I attend meetings at NBC and elsewhere in which people of high rank and station, with salaries to match, say almost nothing else.

For a while I thought it clever to ask people who were spattering me with Y'knows why, if I knew, they were telling me? After having lunch alone with some regularity, I dropped the question. In Britain, a National Society for the Suppression of Y'know, Y'know, Y'know in the Diction of Broadcasters was organized in 1969. It put out a list of the broadcasters who were the worst offenders. Reporters then interviewed the offenders and quoted all the Y'knows in their answers when they were asked whether they really said Y'know that often. Nothing changed.

Once it takes its grip, Y'know is hard to throw off. Some people collapse into Y'know after giving up trying to say what they mean. Others scatter it broadside, these, I suspect, being for some reason embarrassed by a silence of any duration during which they might be suspected of thinking about what they were going to say next. It is not uncommon to hear Y'know used a dozen times in a minute.

We know less about the origin of Y'know than about the origin of Boola boola, but there is some reason to believe that in this country it began among poor blacks who, because of the various disabilities imposed on them, often did not speak well and for whom Y'know was a request for assurance that they had been understood. From that sad beginning it spread, among people who wanted to show themselves sympathetic to blacks, and among those who saw it as the latest thing and either could not resist or did not want to be left out.

Those who wanted to show that they were down to earth, and so not above using Y'know, or — much the same thing — telling you that somebody is like six feet tall, have been particularly influential. They include makers of television commercials who begin the sales pitch with Y'know, and so gain the confidence of the viewer, who realizes at once that the person doing the commercial is down to earth, regular, not stuck-up, and therefore to be trusted.

It also included, on May 1, 1970, the day after he announced the American and South Vietnamese invasion of Cambodia, President Nixon. To a gathering of employes at the Pentagon, he made these remarks about antiwar students at universities:

"You see these bums, you know, blowing up the campuses. Listen, the boys that are on the college campuses today are the luckiest people in the world, going to the greatest universities, and here they are burning up the books, storming around about this issue. You name it. Get rid of

the war and there will be another one."
The White House Watergate transcripts show Mr. Nixon to be fairly devoted to Y'know, even without one use deleted by the White House but shown in the House Judiciary Committee's version: "One of these blacks, y'know, goes in there and holds up a store with a Goddamn gun, and they give him two years and then probation afterward."

The technique might be extended to other fields, perhaps to make Shakespeare more popular in the schools.

HAMLET: To be or not to be, that is the question. Y'know?

Or: I pledge, y'know, allegiance to the flag, and to the y'know, republic for which it stands. One nation indivisible, like I mean with liberty and justice for all. Y'know?

The White House transcript did not show it, but the President also dropped the g at the end of some ing words, apparently to ensure that his down-to-earthness would be recognized.* The g at

* Mr. Nixon supplied another and even less graceful

31

the end of ing words must be thought by politicians to have class connotations that may offend the masses of voters. For that reason it is often dropped in party songs. In 1960, for example, the Democrats' song was "Walkin' Down to Washington," and the Republicans had one about "The Good Time Train," which was "a-waitin' at the station" in the first stanza and "a-waitin' for the nation" in the second.

To choose a lower order of speech is, I suppose, antiestablishment in motive and carries a certain scorn for organized, grammatical, and precise expression. Object to it and you are likely to be told that you are a pedant, a crank, an elitist, and behind the times. "Right on,"

---

demonstration of how down to earth and regular he was when he was visited by a former prisoner of war who gave him an American flag he had made while he was in North Vietnam. The President asked about the man's wife and was told that she had divorced him during his stay in prison camp. Mr. Nixon assured the former prisoner that he would be popular at Washington dinner parties, and added, "Watch out for some of those dogs they have you sit by." Mr. Nixon quickly thought better of this and said, "No, there are some very nice girls in Washington."

"uptight," and "chicken out," to take only a few examples, are looked upon as vivid phrases that enrich and renew the language.

They do enrich it, but they are exhausted very rapidly by overuse. When that happens they wrinkle into clichés before our eyes. Nor does it matter where they come from. "Right on" was a black expression. "It's a new ball game" came from sports. "In orbit" came from the space program. Space was also indirectly responsible for "A nation that can put a man on the moon ought to be able to . . ." Since July 20, 1969, this has been popular with those urging the government to improve mass transit, take care of old people, take care of children, take care of the sick, win the Winter Olympics, win the Summer Olympics, build a nonpolluting automobile engine, see to it that meat in supermarkets is wrapped in packages transparent on both sides, and so on and so on. Those who say these things believe that they have put forward compelling ideas, and such pronouncements do often pass for thought. In reality they camouflage its absence.

Much written and spoken expression these days is equivalent to the background music that incessantly encroaches on us, in banks, restaurants, department stores, trains, shops, airports, airplanes, dentists' offices, hospitals, elevators, waiting rooms, hotel lobbies, pools, apartment building lobbies, bars, and, to my personal knowledge, at least one museum. It thumps and tinkles away, mechanical, without color, inflection, vigor, charm, or distinction. People who work in the presence of background music often tell you, and sometimes with pride, that they don't hear it anymore. The parallel with language is alarming.

Language, then, sets the tone of our society. Since we must speak and read, and spend much of our lives doing so, it seems sensible to get some pleasure and inspiration from these activities. The wisecrack is a wonderful thing, and the colorful phrase, and the flight of fancy. So is the accurate description of a place or an event, and so is the precise formulation of an idea. They brighten the world.

It need not be elaborate. In January, 1974, during the struggle over wages between the British miners' union and the government, there was speculation that Prime Minister Edward Heath would call an election. A BBC man went out to interview miners:

BBC MAN: Do you want an election?

MINER: Yes.

BBC MAN: Why?

MINER: To get the buggers out.

In March, 1958, I was in Tunis to cover a speech by President Bourguiba about Tunisian independence. I started to leave the building where the speech was being made, and a policeman told me that if I did, I could not get back in.

NEWMAN: Mais je suis journaliste.

POLICEMAN: Oui, monsieur, et moi, je suis policier.

I stayed.

In the summer of 1966 I attended a concert in the Alhambra in Granada as the guest of Andrés Segovia. A pianist played a Beethoven concerto with the

Madrid Symphony and received polite applause. At once he sat down and played an encore. Segovia leaned over to me. "Too queeck," he said.

Maestro!

Most of us will never speak that succinctly or concretely. We may, however, aspire to. For direct and precise language, if people could be persuaded to try it, would make conversations more interesting, which is no small thing; it would help to substitute facts for bluster, also no small thing; and it would promote the practice of organized thought and even of occasional silence, which would be an immeasurable blessing.

I do not want to overstate the case. The rules of language cannot be frozen and immutable; they will reflect what is happening in society whether we want them to or not. Moreover, just as libraries, which are storehouses of wisdom, are also storehouses of unwisdom, so will good English, being available to all, be enlisted in evil causes. Still, it remains true that since nothing is more important to a society than the language it uses — there would be no society without it — we would be better off if we spoke and wrote with exactness and grace, and if we preserved, rather than destroyed, the value of our language.

It is not as complicated as it is sometimes made out to be. At an English girls' school one of the mistresses was asked whether the children were allowed to have comic books. She cited no studies, surveys, or research projects. "Oh, no," she said. "Such inferior language."

I speak, then, for a world from which the stilted and pompous phrase, the slogan and the cliché, have not been banished — that would be too much to hope for — but which they do not dominate. This book is intended to help bring about, good-naturedly, I hope (please, not hopefully), that outcome.

1

Hopefully, Fit to Print

In American journalism we have created no legend to compare with Lunchtime O'Booze, star reporter for the British satirical magazine *Private Eye*. It may be because we also have no journalistic practices as old-fashioned and outrageous as those still engaged in by some British papers — "I Fly to the Flashpoint Island," "Fare Shock!" "Airline Chaos Faces Holiday Thousands" (a clear favorite among British headline writers, perhaps because of envy), and "Lisbon, Thursday: The heady wine of revolution flows freely in the streets of Lisbon tonight as citizens uncork the bottles and hand them to the rebel troops who toppled

Prime Minister Marcello Caetano in a one-day coup.'' With these real-life models, Lunchtime coaxes many a rousing story from his battered but sturdy portable:

I SEE SINAI HELL-HOLE HORROR

Make no mistake, this is war! Today with my own eyes I saw the holocaust that is turning the Middle East into a bloodbath that puts the Red Sea to shame. Just what is going on, it was hard to make out. But one thing is certain. This is war. Even the normally tight-lipped Israeli generals are openly admitting it.

FEAR STALKS PARADISE ISLE

Today I saw with my own eyes the stark terror which overnight has turned this paradise on earth into a living nightmare. They are calling it The Island of Death — this international playground for millionaires and sun-seekers alike. The question everyone here is asking is: Why did it have to happen here on this exotic sun-drenched haven hideaway?

I CALL IT LONDON'S
DAY OF SHAME!

Hell on four wheels! That was the picture yesterday as London ground to a halt in what a [Royal Automobile Club] spokesman described as "the worst snarl-up in the entire history of the world."

All over central London, the scene of chaos was the same, as tens of thousands of motorists battled their way to and from work in a sea of frustration and fury. Tempers boiled over and fists were raised as normally sober citizens were reduced by London's Day of Shame to what a High Court judge described as nothing more than a pack of wild animals.

American journalism is, however, not without its resources, and the hack phrase, the labored point, and the stereotyped treatment are by no means unknown, and Lunchtime O'Booze would not scorn the columnist Joseph Alsop.

In May, 1974, Alsop wrote a column

headed, "The Undiluted Horror That Lies Ahead." The undiluted horror lay ahead four times in the column, once for an interminable period, and horror unundiluted lay ahead once. The United States government was described as paralyzed by Watergate four times (this *was* the undiluted horror) and also as being in the vulnerable state of a beached whale and afflicted by Watergate mania (twice) with the result that what the government was doing about anything was "zero," which "profoundly imperiled" all America's interests overseas and all America's friends overseas.

"Altogether," Alsop concluded, "if the undiluted horror does not lead to far greater disasters, it will be proof that this country is in God's own care."

Lunchtime, look to your laurels.

Here is a story from the *New York Times:*

"Moscow, Nov. 5 — Marshal Boris P. Bugayev, the Soviet Minister of Civil Aviation, personally directed the successful foiling of an attempt to hijack a Soviet domestic airliner to Sweden last

Friday, unofficial sources said today."

The story went on from there, but it never did tell us how close Bugayev came to unsuccessfully foiling the attempt to hijack the airliner.

I do not recall seeing a report of a successful foiling before that one in the *Times* in 1973. The phrase had, however, a certain inevitability about it, the way having been paved by totally destroyed, completely destroyed, surrounded on three sides, partially surrounded, completely surrounded, partially damaged, completely abandoned, completely eliminated, most unique, rather unique, very unique, and totally unique.

Think back to Victorian melodrama. The villain has tied the heroine to the railroad track as the express approaches. This is part of his revenge on the hero. The hero, however, arrives in the nick of time, frees the girl, and rolls with her to safety as the train thunders by. The villain gnashes his teeth over this safe escape. "Successfully foiled again," he mutters as the curtain falls.

The Associated Press from San Francisco, February 14, 1971:

"Marathon talks continued today in an effort to end an eight-day strike of city employes that has paralyzed public transit."

Marathon talks are a relatively new development in labor negotiations. As the representatives of employer and union pound along, gasping out proposals about wage differentials and grievance procedures, and accusing each other of not engaging in genuine collective bargaining, the virtue of marathon talks becomes clear. It is that the parties quickly tire of the pace and, rather than go on running, come to an agreement. Even if they keep going, an artfully placed last ditch is provided for them to fall into, and these last-ditch talks avert, as last-ditch talks will, a costly walkout. It is a more effective and healthier method than the one so often recommended by irate citizens, locking them in a room until they come up with a contract.

Marathon talks may, however, lead to

less than equitable results. If the employer representative finds the going hard, and is clearly winded, he may have to yield a whopping wage increase to get some rest. Whenever this happens, it raises one of the most intriguing questions in American journalism: When does an increase being to whop? There is a school of thought among economists that this takes place unfailingly between ninety and one hundred twenty days of inflation beginning to soar. Historically, however, the determination has been left to the discretion of individual reporters and has never been firmly established.

Foreign journalists are not without sin, and it was on the BBC that I heard a reference to Bach's taxing Goldberg Variations, though in a government of laws, not men, the ways of taxing Goldberg are no more numerous than the ways of taxing anyone else. When I was stationed in Rome in the late 1950s, archeologists dug up the mummy of a female thought to be about twenty centuries old. The story at once went out that it was the mummy of a beautiful young woman, and there was speculation about how she came to be there — died for love, buried alive by an ardent tyrant to whom she refused to yield (the proper journalistic phrase for this is Slain for Love), all the usual sort of thing. Experts were called in to analyze the remains and concluded that it was the skeleton of a nine-year-old girl with rickets.

The following story was carried by the AP on October 5, 1973:

"Buenos Aires, Argentina — AP: A high-ranking police officer was shot to death in front of his home Thursday night in the fourth political murder since Juan D. Peron was elected President less than two weeks ago."

Juan D. Peron. The D. is there to keep you from confusing Juan D. Peron with the Juan Q. Peron also elected president of Argentina two weeks earlier. It is there as well because wire services love middle initials. So do newspapers and news magazines. So do television networks. Middle initials are thought to add authenticity and the ring of history. That is why they are so often heard in nominating speeches at party conventions. That is why, when newspapers call on Presiden Nixon to resign, they always specify that it is President Richard M. Nixon they have in mind.

The desire for weightiness even creeps into the language of television weather forecasters. In Denver one night, after the local newscaster had said that something had been done "as best as possible," he referred to an "alleged shoot-out," which not merely was alleged but had taken place, with three people killed. The alleged probably was intended to cover the fact that there was a dispute over who should be prosecuted for it. With that, however, our newscaster reached familiar ground, turned brightly to the weatherman, and asked, "Will we have more major thunderstorm activity?"

The weatherman spotted the cue and, with equal spontaneity and an unerring instinct for the lively phrase, replied, "You better believe it, Ron. That is the prospect," he continued, "as of right now."

I long ago stopped wondering why major thunderstorm activity is preferred to major thunderstorms. It is because of the national affection for unnecessary word activity. Once upon a time, weathermen spoke of showers. (I heard one of them say, "We may have a scattered shower.") Showers were succeeded by shower activity. More recently, the shower area has taken over. All this has happened because we love to pump air into the language and make it soft and gaseous. Newmen borrow the style from those they consider authoritative, such as the air-force general who talked one day about the nuclear deterrent and how well it deterred. It deterred so well, the general said, that the Russians were not in a position to attack us with any confidence factor. The general did not say the Russians lacked confidence. They lacked a confidence factor.

In the same way, head winds no longer delay commercial airliners. Head wind components do. They don't blow at any more miles an hour than head winds do, but a wind is only a wind, while a component is knowledgeable and has know-how. Psychologists no longer speak of children playing but of children in a play situation. My daughter, when she was doing social work, heard it said of a child that he had "not mastered the reading situation." People burying their dead are now said to be in an acute grief situation, and funeral pre-planning is recommended as a way of helping them to deal with it.

Television sportcasters do it, too. They do not say that a team is forced to punt but that it is in a punting situation. A phrase like "punting situation" need be used only once and hordes of journalists descend on it and make it their own. Somebody once described a legal brief as lengthy. Now there is no other kind. There is no record of anybody's ever submitting a short brief, or brief brief. Lengthy is automatic, like powerful before Ways and Means Committee, and all-important before Rules Committee, and uneasy before truce.

When President Nixon announced the

agreement for the separation of Egyptian and Israeli forces along the Suez Canal after the fighting in October, 1973, he remarked that the recent history of the Middle East had been one of outbreaks of fighting, each of them succeeded by an uneasy truce.* True enough. But who ever heard of an easy truce, or a comfortable one? If one did turn up, it would escape notice, because reporters would not be sent to cover it. They go to the Middle East because it is a tinderbox filled with fertile soil (in spite of its being oil-rich) in which an uneasy truce may grow.

* Mr. Nixon missed a bet here by not speaking of the oil-rich Middle East, but we all slip up occasionally. He had begun sounding like a commentator much earlier, when he was out of office in the 1960s. My impression was that he did this to emphasize his already long experience and the positions he had held, so as to set himself above his rivals. In May, 1967, he held a news conference in Chicago and said that the Republicans would have more candidates for the presidential nomination than either party had had in the century. He listed a number of "potential candidates" in addition to those generally known. He noted that some people regarded him as a candidate. Then he said that the Republicans would win and, commentating harder than ever,

49

Later, if an uneasy truce has held up, the same reporters will probably be present when the parties to it sit down to negotiate. This process could be interrupted by setbacks, during which the negotiations grind to a halt and each side spells out its minimum demands (m-i-n-i-m-u-m d-e-m-a-n-d-s) and insists that all it wants is a settlement that will be viable

forecast a photo finish.

A week earlier Mr. Nixon had returned from a tour of Latin America. The picture there, he said, offering what I suppose must be called commentation, was of "a desperate race between production and population." With that, he began sounding like a television newsman on one of the year-end programs, when he reports on his area and makes a prediction. "Castro is waging unrelenting verbal warfare against the unstable regimes of Latin America," Mr. Nixon said. "There will be some rocky roads and some explosion points. The next few years will tell the tale." Becoming president did not change Mr. Nixon. On October 26, 1973, after a cease fire had been established between Egypt and Syria on the one side and Israel on the other, he held a news conference which included "A very significant and potentially explosive crisis," and "My up-to-the-minute report on that — and I just talked to Dr. Kissinger five minutes before coming down — is this." He did everything but promise to be back after this message.

and that the ball is in the other side's court. At this point the scenario (30 LASHES 30 would be an appropriate punishment for anybody using *that* word) calls for globe-trotting diplomat Henry Kissinger (H-e-n-r-y K-i-s-s-i-n-g-e-r) to arrive. Kissinger, who habitually carries heavy objects on his person while trotting, even when wearing more than one hat, gives a hammer to each side. Both take the cue, whereupon an agreement is hammered out.

As automatic as uneasy before truce was Marxist before the title of the late President Allende of Chile. You would have thought that Marxist President was the position Allende had run for and been elected to.

An earlier specimen of Marxist President was Walther Ulbricht of East Germany. His full name, actually, was Spade-bearded Walther Ulbricht, but an odd thing happened as he grew older. His first name changed from Spade-bearded to Aging, possibly — since he was a well-known puppet of Moscow — out of deference to the aging Soviet Politburo.

Ulbricht would sometimes meet other prominent politicians whose first names were Balding and Left-leaning.

In addition to Marxist President, a political office that sometimes has to be filled is that of Ailing Premier. Openings in this position often occur in Japan, probably because the incumbents, given the condition they are required to be in to get the job — i.e., ailing — rarely finish their terms. If they are in particularly frail health, a meeting with somebody who holds the position of Right-wing Strongman in another country may finish them; so may trouble at home with the holder of the post of Balky Defense Minister; and of course, for anybody who is Aging and Ailing at the same time, the end cannot be far off. For example, in Vientiane, in 1962, I met Right-wing Laotian Strongman Phoumi Nosavan, who shortly thereafter turned out to be Right-wing Laotian Weakman Phoumi Nosavan instead.

When politicians called Aging, Ailing, and even Left-leaning* go abroad, they

* Senator Robert Dole once called former Attorney

52

stay in swank hotels which they prefer to Hiltons and others. In New York, they may leave their swank hotels for a visit to the United Nations' posh headquarters. Posh headquarters reveal themselves not only by their poshness but by having been built with public money. Headquarters built with private money, even for prestigious law firms, do not qualify.

Foreign leaders may also, if their tastes run that way, visit a sprawling installation or two. The sprawling Marshall Space Flight Center in Huntsville, Alabama, is among those available, and there are countless others, equally ungraceful, including the sprawling ethyl plant in Baton Rouge, Louisiana. Wives of foreign leaders may visit sprawling shopping centers.

Having visited the world organization at its posh headquarters, the foreign leader may go to Washington to call on the chief executive, or the embattled chief executive, if *he* happens to be in office. If

---

General Ramsey Clark a left-leaning marshmallow. Clark's reply, if any, is not recorded.

the visitor is unpopular, there may be demonstrations against him, with the television reporters explaining that "The demonstrators were protesting alleged repressive measures in his homeland." If the police are called in, there may soon thereafter be reports of demonstrators protesting alleged police brutality. In some countries, where customs are different, demonstrators, frequently university students, may instead rampage through appropriate neighborhoods and buildings while protesting alleged government corruption. This, as the UPI told us, was the case in Patna, India, in March, 1974. Anybody who rampages is inviting alleged repression with concomitant alleged police brutality.

Back, however, to the meeting between the foreign leader and the chief executive. When they meet, the mysterious corps of diplomatic observers, its whereabouts known only to correspondents who cover foreign policy matters, goes into action. Two kinds of diplomatic observers are available, ordinary and seasoned. The situation being dealt with here — foreign leader in wide-ranging parley with chief executive — is fairly straightforward and does not warrant disturbing the seasoned diplomatic observers. Ordinary diplomatic observers suffice, and they cease observing ordinarily long enough to tell reporters covering the story that the top-level meeting is necessary to prevent a situation already difficult from escalating into an eyeball-to-eyeball confrontation.

In the early days of American involvement in Vietnam, after Lyndon Johnson had faced Aging Mao Tse-tung eyeball-to-eyeball in the Gulf of Tonkin and had shown him to be a paper tiger by making the Chinese leader blink — blinking in such confrontations being the infallible sign of a paper-tigerness — I remarked on the air that an eyeball-to-eyeball confrontation between Johnson and Mao must have been difficult to arrange, given the considerable difference in height and eye shapes. A professor in California at once wrote to accuse me of a racist attempt to whip up anti-Chinese feeling. I blinked.

I took part in a television program in which Senator Henry Jackson, describing the somewhat faltering progress of the détente between the Soviet Union and the United States, described the situation as half-an-eyeball-to-half-an-eyeball. Presumably, if things improved, the half-an-eyeball confrontation would give way to confrontation by peripheral vision, and finally, on the bright sunlit uplands of peace, the two parties would not be looking at each other at all.

Eyeball-to-eyeball, though it came close to burlesque even at the beginning (for example, when hard-nosed private eyes are private-eyeball-to-private-eyeball, does eye or nose prevail?), was once a fairly graphic phrase. Because of overuse, it has been devalued. American journalism has a way of seeing to that, of fastening on words and sucking them dry. Controversial is such a word, because it is applied to almost every issue that arises in politics, and because reporters feel obliged to tell us that issues that are resolved in the Senate by votes of fifty-one to forty-nine are controversial. Again, as anyone can discern from book jackets, scarcely a book appears that is not controversial, even when it is also witty, warm, and wise.

The television critic of the *New York Times,* John O'Connor, recently shed some light on *The Merchant of Venice* by describing Shylock as controversial. Macbeth was, too, of course: some say it was his fault, some say it was his wife's.

Nelson Rockefeller explained why his Commission on Critical Choices would not ask the federal government for money: "Like anything in these days of controversy, this commission, privately organized, got into a controversial situation. We decided not to pursue a request for funding from either the Executive or Congress. It was bound to be controversial."

I in turn regarded Rockefeller's decision as controversial, but it is his commission, and he can do what he likes with it.

Meanwhile has gone the same way that controversial has; it now serves about as much purpose as a clearing of the throat.

Massive has also, and here the matter is more serious. Massive was robbed of its original meaning, which is to say forming a large mass, heavy, bulky, solid, so that it could be used to mean large, a word considered no longer able to stand on its own but requiring size after it. Massive doesn't even mean large anymore. It goes by without registering. It means nothing.

Still worse is the destruction of rhetoric. Rhetoric does not mean fustian, exaggeration, or grand and empty phrases. It means — it meant — the effective use of language, and the study of that use. Suddenly beloved of politicians and journalists, rhetoric is now used to mean something doubtful and not quite honest, instead of something desirable. Its misapplication could hardly tell more than it does. The director of the Center for Russian and East European Studies at the University of Michigan, William Zimmerman, has written of someone's "rhetorical thrust." This is a veritable synthesis.

Not only words become hackneyed. People do too. As long ago as October,

1951, while working in London, I invented the Winkfield Award, given for journalistic achievement above and beyond the call of duty. I wrote about it in *Punch:*

I never thought the day would come when I'd interview my old friend Dymchurch. He and I had made our modest starts in journalism together, and for a while he was no more prominent than I, which is to say not prominent at all. Even recently he hadn't seemed to me to be doing anything out of the ordinary, and then, to my surprise, came his winning of the Winkfield Journalism Award for outstanding public service.

"It's an old story," he told me, "a cliché. I started low and worked up. Of course I didn't realize it at the time, but looking back now I can see exactly how it began. It was my not interviewing somebody who won seventy-five thousand pounds in a football pool. That gave me my start.

"You can't plan these things," he

went on. "It was pure accident, and so was the next step — not interviewing a woman who, in response to a newspaper advertisement, was about to travel five thousand miles to marry a man she'd never seen.

"Up to then, it was fairly routine stuff," he continued, "but it was the sort of experience that helps later on. You may recall that I became a war correspondent. I got to Chungking, and it was there that I never interviewed Chou En-lai. Later the opportunity arose of not interviewing Mao Tse-tung in a cave in Yenan."

"Which you took?" I asked.

"Oh, yes," he said, smiling with satisfaction. "By that time I was firmly on the road. Soon after, I did not submit a list of written questions to Stalin. War corresponding was a highly competitive business, you know. You have no idea what that did for my prestige."

"After hitting the high spots that way," I said, "it must have been difficult for you when the war ended."

"It was," he said. "I had to keep my

hand in by not asking American tourists how they liked it here, and not asking G.I. brides who came back to see their families how they liked it there. It wasn't much but it kept me from getting rusty. Then things took a turn for the better, and I was able not to interview Communists who changed their minds."

"So you were ready when the big chance came?" I asked.

"Absolutely," he said emphatically. "That's how I won the award. I told myself it was now or never, and then I went out and did not interview Tito. I don't like to boast, but I ask you, in all honesty, how many journalists, or non-journalists, for that matter, can make that claim?"

I admitted it was very few.

"Of course," he went on expansively, "there are some people who believe that the non-interview of Tito was not the best thing I've done. They think that came later, with my not interviewing Mossadegh at his bedside. They may be right. I confess I don't know which I prefer myself. But the Winkfield people seem more impressed by the Tito thing. It was a bit of a coup."

"I suppose," I said, "that you feel there are no more worlds for you to conquer."

"There is that problem," he said. "But something always turns up. The big thing is to be ready for it." He lowered his voice. "You're an old friend," he said. "I can trust you. I've got something up my sleeve. I've noticed a few interviews with General Franco lately. That sounds like the beginning. I think an opportunity is building up there. It's a question of timing. I'll let a few months go by and then I'll do my stuff."

His eyes lit up, and he rubbed his hands gleefully. "It could be my greatest triumph," he said.

In that piece for *Punch* I was wrong. Franco never allowed himself to become an easy interview subject. The days of Tito, Mossadegh (prime minister of Iran, 1951 - 53, nationalizer of the Iranian oil industry, usually interviewed propped up in bed and wearing pajamas), and, later, Gamal Abdel Nasser in Egypt, were heady days for seekers of the Winkfield Award and were never equaled. In our own time, some have made a stab at comparable glory. They have never asked for comment from men in the street, strasse, rue, calle, piazza, or prospekt. They did not interview Princess Anne at the time of her wedding; they did not interview Captain Mark Phillips; and they did not interview Princess Anne and Captain Mark Phillips together. One journalist, a woman of original mind, refrained from interviewing Abba Eban and then, understandably keyed up, in quick succession did not question the reigning Federal Energy Czar and made no attempt to draw out Senator Edward Kennedy on his plans for 1976.

Nobody can deny that she deserves well of her countrymen, but hers is still not a winning performance. There are too many people not to interview now. Television has done that, and jet aircraft, and the large number of new countries. The possibilities are endless. Wherefore the Winkfield Award is no more.

It is too bad. I can almost hear the exchange between the award committee chairman and the winner when the trophy is handed over.

"We are all eager to know how you came to refrain from interviewing the Federal Energy Czar. Will you tell us?"

The winner looks weary, as befits one who has been under the strain of not interviewing so many of the world's great figures. "It was," he replies, "because he is there."

"The *New York Times,*" I hear you saying. "Surely the *New York Times* is free of these things. There was that successful foiling of the hijacking, but that must have been an aberration. No?"

No. While the motto of the *Times,* "All the News That's Fit to Print," is not exactly shy and retiring, it is not the news in the *Times* I mean to have at. It is the English. The English is not always fit to print. Far from it.

For long years now, one of the worst things the *Times* has done is to use the construction "convince to." You may convince that. You may convince of. You may not convince to. Unfortunately, this use has caught on and is now virtually accepted. There is no more chance of heading it off than there is of preserving media as a plural. Someone should convince the *Times* that it will bear a large part of the blame.

Here is an editorial in which the *Times* remarks that the Soviet Union "evidently is not able to convince Cairo to accept a rapid cease-fire." Here is a story about the tenor Richard Tucker, who wanted to sing *La Juive* but "was unable to convince Rudolf Bing to stage the work"; and one about Lockheed hoping "to convince airlines to accept modifications of its basic model — the L-1011-1 — that would give it transatlantic range"; and one about a new cigarette filter that Columbia University became interested in, in which the *Times* speaks of convincing heavy smokers to cut down their smoking.

The *Times* was not exclusively to blame for the last one, because Columbia

University itself, in its press release about the filter, said, "It may be impossible to convince many people to stop smoking." Maybe Columbia should filter its press releases through its English Department.

If the *Times* can do it, why not others?

United Press International from Ankara:

"Two U. S. Congressmen tried to convince Turkey today to reconsider its decision to resume cultivation of the opium poppy, source of heroin."

Associated Press, from Philadelphia:

"A group of University of Pennsylvania students has called for a 'streak for impeachment' April 1 around the White House.

"They say they are hoping to convince President Nixon to 'lay bare the facts' about Watergate."

Time magazine, March 25, 1974:

"Ervin was aided by Paul Verkuil, a professor at the University of North Carolina, in gathering the evidence that convinced Congress to adopt the provision."

In any case, why do people say — and, more particularly, journalists write — "He was convinced to withdraw his candidacy"? Only a few years ago they would have correctly said, "He was persuaded to." Why, further, do so many people say comprised of instead of composed of? Composed of filled the bill for a very long time. Why, after centuries, has more importantly, misused, begun to replace more important? The *Times* does nothing to resist it: "There has been a gradual shift, over the past 25 years, in the balance of economic power, and even more importantly, in the attitudes governing the relationships between the United States and her neighbors in the Western Hemisphere." "More importantly, in getting kids to read, the impulse to 'read the book, see the movie' works both ways." The ultimate: "Most importantly, he would like to help in prisons." It has, naturally, made its way into commercials, so that it is said of a Guerlain spray, "More importantly, it travels." More importantly, more unfortunately, does too.

What makes the incorrect more attractive than the correct? Gresham's Law tells us that the less valuable currency will force the more valuable out of circulation. That, however, does not explain the case; it merely states it. There is at work here the desire to be up with the latest in thing. But that leaves the question of how the latest in thing came to be. People say, "Hopefully, something will happen." They could, as they did for so long, use the simple and straightforward, "I hope." They don't say, "Hopelessly, nothing will happen." Why should James Reston write in the *Times,* ". . . we are left to our instincts and emotions, and hopefully to our common sense"? Why does the *Times* write, "Hopefully, the Americans believe that this would increase the chances for a peaceful resolution of the Arab-Israeli conflict"? Is it a hope or belief the Americans have? Or is it that the *Times* hopes the Americans believe it? Maybe in the scramble of daily journalism there isn't time to catch these things. But why should Robert Alan Aurthur write ". . . if the city fell apart from a simple power failure, soon hopefully to be repaired, what would happen in the event of a real disaster?'' and why should *Esquire,* a monthly, accept it?

Why do American politicians invariably say ''I would hope''? (''Right now we are experiencing rather critical shortages in various parts of states, most of it centered on the east coast. I would hope our allocation program would take care of that.'' — William Simon.) They never specify the conditions under which their hoping would come to pass.

Vice-President Ford said, ''I would hope that the White House would cooperate,'' about the tapes the House Judiciary Committee wanted from President Nixon. (Otherwise, he said, there might be a head-to-head confrontation, this being one in which the eyeballs face the ground while the tops of the skulls are in contact.)

British politicians go a step further. They say ''I would have hoped,'' which implies a wistful detachment. Wistful detachment has not been a recommended attitude for American politicians since the days of Adlai Stevenson, so we may be spared this.

When — and more to the point, why — did a troop become the same thing as a soldier? A troop is a body of men. This, from the *Times* in February, 1974, on the fighting in the Moslem insurgency in the Philippines, is the sort of thing that has become common: "The government admits to more than 300 dead, giving a 'body count' of 225 rebels, about 50 civilians and only 29 of its own troops."

Suppose the casualties were one, one, and one. Would the report then speak of a body count of one rebel, one civilian, and one troop? If *Times* foreign affairs columnist C. L. Sulzberger were writing it, perhaps not. "There are still," he wrote in March, 1974, "about 313,000 U. S. forces in Europe's defense, of whom 190,000 are ground troops in Germany." Sulzberger might make it one rebel, one civilian, and one force.

Here are other tidbits from recent issues of the *Times:* "Equally as costly."

Equally as is redundant. "As for example." Redundant. "Different than," rather than different from, is wrong. So is "augur for." Augur does not take for after it. It cannot take for after it. Also, ". . . anyone who feels that either Sills or Lorengar are milking the piece for more than it is worth . . ." Most critics felt that neither soprano were, though in other music, each perhaps do. "Both men had worked together at the Columbia Broadcasting System." On the well-known man-bites-dog principle, the *Times* should have reported this only if one man had worked together at CBS. In the 1973 American League playoff, the *Times* had Jim Palmer of Baltimore and Vida Blue of Oakland engaging in a "flaunted pitching classic." It could have been worse. It could have been flouted.

Not long ago the *Times* put an advertisement in the *Times* for its own help-wanted columns. The advertisement said: "Are you a housewife and have the time to earn extra money while enjoying a change of pace? A temporary job may be the answer." A suitable reply would have been: "No, I aren't have the time to earn extra money while enjoying a change of pace. Are you?"

A headline: "Clean Air Likely to Cost Taxpayer." One in arrears, I trust. From James Reston, a reference to a serious economic crisis facing Egypt. For the Egyptians' sake, I hope so. A serious crisis is the only kind to have. Crises that are not serious are not worth the trouble. It's like the true facts politicians so often demand or, conversely, insist that they are giving us. True facts are the only facts worth having. False facts are no use at all, a point that escaped a State Department spokesman who said of an article in *Foreign Policy*: "Some of the facts are true, some are distorted, and some are untrue." True facts, in (true) fact, are like the factual numbers to which William Simon was devoted as Federal Energy Czar. Nonfactual numbers don't count.

When Alexander Solzhenitsyn arranged for the publication of his account of Soviet prison camps, *The Gulag Archipelago,* in Paris in December, 1973, the *Times* reported that the Soviet government was in a dilemma. Doing nothing would show it to be ineffective, while "The other horn of the dilemma," the *Times* pointed out, seeing to the heart of the matter, "is equally unattractive." A dilemma has to get up pretty early in the morning to fool the *New York Times*.

In March, 1974, the *Times* reported an attack by *Pravda,* the Soviet Communist party newspaper, on Secretary of State Kissinger. The *Times* began by describing *Pravda* as authoritative, which it certainly is. Then it quoted *Pravda* as saying that in Kissinger's Middle East negotiations, "the mountain produced a mouse." The *Times,* thinking this cryptic, added, "an allusion to the Aesopian fable about monumental efforts producing pitifully small results." Always helpful, the *Times*.

When Ibsen's *A Doll's House* was about to open in New York, the *Times* had an article about a rehearsal. It began, "The cast was a half hour late for rehearsal and Patricia Elliott, one of the few to arrive early, was waxing ecstatically about the new set." The *Times* thereby created a picture of Miss Elliott happily shining the furniture on the theater stage, presumably after an agreement between Actors Equity and the Stagehands Union.

So it goes. The *Times* has described Cuban peasants as "prone to pressure from the government, the army, and the plantation owners." With those pressures, no wonder the peasants are prone. It has told us of a soprano with a big-sized voice and a dance company that gave "the most number of performances in years," and of a parcel of land that was square-shaped, thereby saving countless people from believing that it was square-colored.

Some mistakes in the *Times* are hard to classify. When Kwame Nkrumah was deposed in Ghana, the *Times* spoke of his "oustering." Maybe it meant his removaling. It banished a blameless baritone to limbo in its review of a Metropolitan Opera performance of *Otello:* "Except for David Holloway, as the Herald, the other members of the cast were William Lewis (Cassio), Jean Kraft (Emilia) and Paul Plishka (Lodovico)."

Look at this sentence: "With frequent disdain for grammar, logic and, often, accuracy, Hedda Hopper produced a Hollywood gossip column for 28 years." The *Times* evidently believed there was a difference between doing something frequently and doing it often. Which leads to an item from Jack Gould's television column: "But particularly intriguing is the possible consequences of the subway strike on Mr. Lindsay's video fortunes." Gould was right. Consequences often is intriguing. Not frequently, perhaps, but often. That's how consequences on video fortunes is.

Sentences like that one came frequently, as well as often, from Gould. There was this about Mia Farrow:

"Miss Farrow is an interesting personality to know more about, and her attempts to articulate her own set of faith and convictions is probably pertinent to comprehending the 'Now Generation.' "

Gould also gave us this:

"In the judgment of some

75

entertainment executives, the relationship between TV and the motion-picture industry has come full circle. The Hollywood tycoons, in the all-time classic misjudgment of show business, at first ignored TV. Then they sold off their libraries. Now they and TV are becoming partners."

That's full circle.

What follows is not Gould, but try it anyway:

"Dr. Nigrelli, and his wife, Margaret, who live at 11 West 183rd Street, the Bronx, is a native of Pittston, Pa."

Past participles trouble the *Times:*

"Mr. Ives portrays the richest man in the world, a widower, who seeked social status for himself and his children."

"J. W. Fulbright, chairman of the committee, plainly indicated he thought Mr. McNamara had treaded close to deception."

". . . an individual who has bestrode American life for a quarter of a century — Eisenhower of Abilene, Normandy and Washington."

From the sports pages of the *Times,* in

an article about Bill Russell at the time he was appointed coach and general manager of the Seattle Supersonics of the National Basketball Association: "This is the second time around for Russell as a coach. As the playing coach of the Celtics for three seasons, Boston won two titles."

That is a non sequitur, as well as a misplaced, dangling modifier, but I suppose that it can be understood as easily as the confused notice now so often seen: "Having left my bed and board, I am no longer responsible for debts incurred by my wife." Or this, from a UPI story about motherly weather in Utah: "After stuffing the apparel in the Cessna 210's windows to keep out the blistering winds, a snowstorm completely covered the craft."

Like many people, the *Times* has trouble with former. A story on the society page said that Leslie J. Leathers, son of the Viscount Leathers "who was a former British Minister of Transport," had announced the engagement of his daughter. This suggests that when Lord Leathers joined the government, the

Prime Minister called him in and said, "Leathers, I hereby appoint you former Minister of Transport." That came later, after he'd had the job for a while.

This line appeared in the *Times*'s news summary one recent March twenty-second: "Despite weather, spring arrives on schedule." This seemed odd, since the arrival of spring is what might be called a predictable event, and there is no case on record of spring's not arriving at the appointed time. The *Times,* however, did not look at it that way. "Spring arrives, despite clouds," it said in a headline on page 27. Any newspaper likes to have an exclusive angle, and the *Times* had one, that if the clouds had been more lowering, or spring less determined, spring would not have made it.

Such developments come thick and fast at the *Times*. The arrival of spring was a key and/or major development in the calendar. In a recent period of three weeks the *Times* conferred keyness on local news; labor and management negotiators (who were also top-level bargainers); Democrats in Congress; an election in West Germany; a cabinet post in Israel; the position of Herbert Kalmbach as a Watergate witness; a British insurance broker and parts of letters he was accused of forging; a piece of evidence in the Watergate affair, against which some witnesses were only potentially key; five initiatives that some Arizona citizens who had joined in a loose coalition wanted to put on the ballot in November; and a problem in the development of solar power.

It ascribed the state of being major to newspapers and print publications; a beneficiary of political maneuvering in Israel who might have been expected to work himself into that position since he had, the *Times* pointed out, a reputation for capability; candidates in the French presidential election; television as a source of news; questions facing President Nixon; crimes; a news story; a military defeat in Cambodia; the reason a referendum on divorce was expected to be a political watershed in Italy; the economy as a political issue; the importance of matters on which Yitzhak

Rabin, as Israeli ambassador to Washington, consulted Golda Meir; a stumbling block in a labor negotiation; guerrilla groups in the Middle East; criticism in the Lebanese parliament; a speech in Moscow on Lenin's birthday; a confrontation between the White House and the Watergate prosecutor; Saudi Arabia; banks; a piece of consumer legislation in Albany; cities; car rental dealers; strategic weapons systems; a study of the Arms Control and Disarmament Agency; the winter oil shortage and price explosion; the collapse in automobile sales and production; the impact of an indictment; issues in Albany; Governor Wilson's presence in Albany; Henry Kissinger's influence on President Sadat of Egypt; an element in the survival of Japanese soldiers recently found alive in the Philippines; a singer from Brittany, in France; recruiting programs for the armed services; the part of the cost of emergency service borne by hospitals; a post office construction program; the role Henry Kissinger allegedly played in investigations of Daniel Ellsberg; a Portuguese resort; industrial countries; a stroke suffered by the son of Emperor Haile Selassie; steel producers; car manufacturers; an American effort to help poor countries; a smallpox area; the revamping of a television news program; the appointment of William Simon as secretary of the treasury; building projects in urban areas; and a function of the educational staff of the Metropolitan Museum of Art.

Then there is spelling. In the *Times* it is sometimes exotic. Maybe I am only knitpicking, as the *Times* had one of Mayor Abe Beame's men saying when his ethics were questioned. Still, the *Times* has had a black-and-white-striped robe flowing majesterially to the floor. It has told us, in a headline, about "India and the Kashmiri shiek," and otherwise has found the teeming subcontinent teeming with orthographic difficulties, so that it used the spelling Ghandi four times in five sentences, hardly a feather in its hatma Gandhi. Dearth has been spelled dirth in the *Times*. Maybe a dirth is an unclean scarcity. Germane has been spelled germain by one of the learned book reviewers. Germane, she cries in vain.

Of course, it isn't only the *Times*. I received a letter a while ago that ended by thanking me in advance for past courtesies, a bit of politesse not unlike something that happened just before one of the Apollo space flights. A box arrived at NBC News in New York with a map in it from the Topographic Command of the United States Army Corps of Engineers in Washington. It was addressed to us at 30 Rockerfellow Plaza.

There are many people who think that Rockefeller is uncouth, a form of dese and dose English. They therefore address us at Rockafellow or Rockerfellow Plaza. As in Nelson Rockafellow, or John D. Rockerfellow III. This package went them one better, however. It carried the warning: "Handel with care." That is good advice. Handel with care. Going Chopin? Liszt with care. Bizet? Take care. Ravel with care. On the other hand, if you are about to unravel, it doesn't matter so much. But Handel with care. Otherwise you might spill the water music.

2

Ongoing Dialogue
vs.
Adversary
Relationship

There are few reputations for eloquence in Washington. Henry Kissinger has one, more or less deserved. His speech is organized, which is to say that it comes out in phrases, sentences, and paragraphs, all apparently premeditated, and that the argument proceeds in an orderly and logical way. Occasionally he is even humorous. Moreover, Kissinger often has an idea that he seeks to communicate; ponderous he may be, but he is genuinely engaged in persuasion.

Such is the astonishment brought on by

a man for whom there is a connection between thought and speech that the reaction is out of proportion. We are told that Kissinger is "majestic," that he has offered "an intellectual tour de force," that he was "at his magisterial best," and so on. In fact — and this is not to belittle Kissinger, who, after all, is not responsible for others — in fact, Kissinger stands out also because of a lack of competition, because the level of most of those around him is so low. It does not take much to be thought eloquent in Washington.

Another beneficiary of this condition is William F. Buckley, Jr. Buckley does not so much speak as exhale, but he exhales polysyllabically, and the results are remarkable. "Epiphenomenon," says Buckley, "epistemology, maieutic," and, so we are led to believe, people swoon all over the nation.

I have sometimes thought that Buckley is considered intellectually imposing because some people, unable otherwise to account for his manner of speech, take him to be English. Many Americans feel themselves inferior in the presence of anyone with an English accent, which is why an English accent has become fashionable in television commercials: it is thought to sound authoritative. Buckley reminds me of a character created by the British comedian Spike Milligan and known as the "pronouner." Looting a bombed-out house during the Second World War, he came upon a dictionary, fell in love with words of many syllables, and devoted the rest of his life to pronouning them. His wife kept the dictionary binding polished, and his work mates waited daily for his latest pronunations. When Buckley pulled out the word anfractuosity to describe the American tax system, I thought of the pronouner. He would have been proud.

Washington — appropriately, since it is the capital of the United States — is the place where language is most thoroughly debased — more than Hollywood, which is not what it used to be; more than the world of advertising, which is; more even than the academic world, a realm of unlimited horizons, in which somebody talking to somebody else is considered to be engaged in information transfer.

A respect for language requires some standards of judgment. In Washington they are lacking. There the chief characteristic of language is self-importance, and it casts its spell quickly. I remember receiving a press release from a first-term congressman headed "Major Policy Statement." He was being as helpful as the producer who tells you that he has made a Major Motion Picture; it saves everybody else the trouble of making up his mind.

Self-importance in Washington begins, naturally, at the White House, and it was an accurate measure of the self-importance that permeated the Nixon White House that the tape-recording system that came to haunt the President should have been put in place. The Johnson administration also had a recording system and at least an equal amount of self-esteem. At the outset of the Kennedy administration, which was bowed down early under a sense of history in the making, an official White House photographer was on the scene incessantly, so that no expression or moment should be lost. Before that, evidently on somebody's sudden inspiration, on January 16, 1961, four days before the inauguration, a telegram went out in some numbers over the signature of President-elect and Mrs. Kennedy:

"During our forthcoming administration we hope to effect a productive relationship with our writers artists composers philosophers scientists and heads of cultural institutions," they said, and went on to say that the recipients of the telegram were invited to attend the inaugural ceremonies "as a beginning in recognition of their importance."

The press, taking its cue from the monarchic our and we, and possibly seeing itself in the role of courtier, soon invoked "Camelot" and "The New Versailles," and talked limitlessly about "style," which had earlier been given a tryout in the days of Adlai Stevenson. Style has since refused to go away, and banks yearning after your money now tell you that they have a thrift style to go with your life style, while sociologists speak of "the legitimacy of mulitiple body styles." This does not mean multiple body styles in a single, or nonmultiple, body. It means it is all right to be fat.

Sometimes reality entirely flees the White House. On October 3, 1966, Nicholas Katzenbach was sworn in as undersecretary of state. Katzenbach had been attorney general, and President Johnson spoke to the television cameras about that. "He has stood here for the cause of freedom," Mr. Johnson said. "He has pursued justice for all Americans. Every man is in his heart."

Then the President spoke about Katzenbach's new post. "Now the scope of his work is the world, and the qualities of mind and spirit which have made him the champion of social change and human progress at home will make him their advocate throughout the world."

There cannot have been many hearts beating faster because Katzenbach was undersecretary of state. But Mr. Johnson did not merely announce his appointments; he congratulated himself on them, and congratulated the nation as well. He made the nomination of an ambassador to Poland sound earth-shaking. Lawrence O'Brien, as the new postmaster general, received such a tribute that it might have seemed he would carry all the mail himself.

The pressure to measure up to such extravagant standards is intense in Washington. President Nixon described the Smithsonian monetary agreement of December, 1971, as the most important agreement of its kind in the history of the world; he described revenue sharing and a guaranteed family income as the second American revolution; and he called the first manned flight to the moon the most important event since the Creation. He must have thought that if he called it epochal nobody would notice. Vice-President Ford, possibly preparing for higher duties, assessed Kissinger's part in the Syrian-Israeli troop disengagement as "the great diplomatic triumph of this century or perhaps any other."

When Campobello Island in Nova Scotia

was given to the Canadian and American governments as a ''peace park'' by the industrialist Armand Hammer and his brother Victor, papers had to be signed by Prime Minister Lester Pearson and President Johnson. A photograph of the ceremony on January 22, 1964, shows the nonsense that has been allowed to grow up around the presidency, for just as words lose their value, so do ceremonies and events. On the left side, Mr. Pearson is signing. He has one pen. On the right side, Mr. Johnson is signing. In front of him sits what looks like a giant punchboard, with pens stuck into it nibs up. As nearly as I could make out, it had spaces for one hundred forty-four pens, plus an inkpot. I don't know how many historic pens Mr. Johnson gave out that day, but at the time the photograph was taken, more than a hundred were in the board.

Pens do something to the American presidential psyche. When President Nixon went to Paris in April, 1974, for the memorial service after the death of President Georges Pompidou, he went out in the street and gave away ball point

91

pens. The French have a word, protocolaire, to describe what is fitting and proper. Giving away pens in such circumstances wasn't.

President Johnson liked things big. The Lyndon B. Johnson Library at the University of Texas in Austin is eight stories high and measures 100,000 square feet. It contains 31,000,000 documents (There's a freighted word! When does a sheet of paper metamorphose into a document?), 500,000 photographs, 500,000 feet of moving-picture film, and 30,000 gifts sent to the Johnsons. With the Lyndon B. Johnson School of Public Affairs at the university, it cost $18,600,000 to build. The cost to the taxpayers of maintaining the library was $540,000 a year at the beginning. It must be more now.

Mr. Johnson was president for more than five years. The Kennedy Library, a memorial to a man who was president for less than three years, threatens to undo an entire neighborhood in Cambridge, Massachusetts, it is to be so big.

Presidential libraries, like many things,

came to a climax of sorts under President Nixon when it turned out that his brother Edward had been retained as a consultant by the Richard Nixon Foundation, a tax-exempt undertaking. Edward Nixon advised the foundation where the Nixon family would like the Nixon presidential library to be, a chore that involved him in consulting himself, and for which he was paid $1,500 a month for fourteen months. According to Leonard Firestone, head of the foundation, Edward visited six sites and recommended that the final selection be made from among three in Orange County, California, an area that might otherwise have escaped attention, since its only claim to consideration was that the President was born and began his legal and political careers there.

About Edward Nixon's compensation Firestone said, "If people think that is too much, let them try to hire a consultant these days and see what they come up with." The plain meaning of that comment was that consultants were becoming so scarce in the United States that low-grade ones had to be used, just as rising prices make low-grade ores economical when they were not economical before. The quality of life is deteriorating in unforeseen and surprising ways.

The Rockefeller brothers, perhaps in expectation, perhaps in aspiration — it's hard to know — have announced plans to build a $4,500,000 archive center holding perhaps 20,000,000 papers related to their family's activities and history. They are to build it on their own land at Pocantico Village, New York, and near their own houses, which will be convenient for popping historic documents into it on the way to and from work.

The outlook for presidential and other libraries is, I am happy to say, cloudy, because in 1969 a law was passed ending tax deductions for the contribution of personal papers to libraries, universities, and the like. Shakespeare said (*The Tempest,* Act II, Scene 1), "What's past is prologue"; we made it for a while, What's past is deductible, but after President Nixon's celebrated and later disallowed $576,000 deduction for his vice-presidential papers (the his is used loosely; it is hard to see how they were his, or how Hubert Humphrey's were Hubert Humphrey's, or those of anybody else in public office those of anybody else in public office), the law is not likely to be repealed.

The papers Mr. Nixon sent to the National Archives in exchange for the $576,000 deduction were 414,000 letters; 87,000 items relating to public appearances, and including speech texts, 27,000 invitations, with acceptances and refusals; and 57,000 items relating to trips abroad. In this mass of materials were newspaper clippings and unclipped newspapers.

I don't know how the stuff Mr. Nixon had delivered to the National Archives, where Shakespeare's line cited above adorns the façade, compares with similar material contributed by others. I think that by rule of thumb — extended in the way the baseball umpire signals "out" — at least 90 percent of it could be thrown away with no loss to anyone. A sense of history and a debt to scholarship are all very well, but how can words and ideas have any value when there are millions of them? The word documents is robbed of meaning when it is claimed that there are 31,000,000 of them.

There is something spooky about the desire to pronounce oneself historic ahead of time. Only history decides on that; anticipation increases the discomforting exaltation we have seen in our recent presidents. It is, for example, expressed in the weighty announcement, "Ladies and gentlemen, the President of the United States," and the playing of "Hail to the Chief." No doubt, if an actress about to receive an award can be serenaded with "A Pretty Girl Is Like a Melody," a president can have "Hail to the Chief" proclaim his arrival. But it does lend an aura of destiny to the daily round when it is hard enough for a president to maintain a sense of proportion, and it might be worse still if presidents knew the words of the song, which come for Sir Walter Scott's "Lady of the Lake":

Hail to the chief, who in triumph
  advances,
Honor'd and blessed be the evergreen
  pine!
Long may the tree in his banner that
  glances,
Flourish, the shelter and grace of our
  line.
Hail to the chief, who in triumph
  advances,
Honor'd and bless'd be the evergreen
  pine!
Long may the tree in his banner that
  glances,
Flourish, the shelter and grace of our
  line.
Heav'n send it happy dew,
Earth lend it sap anew;
Gaily to burgeon and broadly to grow;
While ev'ry highland glen,
Sends our shout back again,
Roderigh Vich Alpine dhu, ho!
  i-e-roe!

Not much has been heard lately about
former Senator John Williams,
Republican of Delaware, who was

responsible for the 1969 law ending deductions for personal papers. I would like to put up a memorial to him, but I am afraid somebody would want to put documents in it. I speak as one who for two years took deductions of $4,215 and $1,340 for papers contributed to the Wisconsin State Historical Society. This also was ridiculous.

The project for a Nixon presidential library is in abeyance and, because of Watergate, may never come to anything. However, Mr. Nixon has announced that he and his wife intend to give their house at San Clemente to the people of the United States. This is the structure that has a sign outside identifying it as the Western White House, which it isn't even though the bills charged to the American people could have confused them into thinking they had bought it, and even though most of the press, in an exercise of self-importance by association, is happy to go along. Nor is the Nixon house in Key Biscayne the Florida White House, any more than Lyndon Johnson's ranch was the Texas White House, though that is what he liked to call it; or John Kennedy's place at Hyannis Port the Cape Cod White House; or the Eisenhower farm the Gettysburg White House. The naval base at Key West, Florida, did not turn into a White House when Harry Truman was there. The White House is in Washington. Presidents do not take it with them when they travel.

Washington is the seat of government because it is where other people in the government sit. If it is objected that presidents are isolated in Washington, a jet flight to Florida or California, followed by a helicopter flight to a guarded compound, is unlikely to remedy that. I am not trying to make the White House a mystic shrine. I am trying to distinguish it from its tenants, who are transient.

It may be that there is something wrong with the White House. Perhaps, with tourists trooping through it, it offers those who live in it no real privacy. For we have seen a strange development in the past few decades. Men dedicate their lives to getting to the White House. What Richard

Nixon went through to get there is almost unimaginable, including Barry Goldwater's saying of him in 1964, "Nixon is sounding more like Harold Stassen every day." Once there, they can hardly wait to leave it. A president is no longer important because he is in the White House but because he is out of it, and the more places at his disposal the better. Likewise the press. It is more glamorous to be not on your regular beat but somewhere else, and it is still more glamorous to be en route.

I know this kind of thing from my own experience. One night during the Suez Crisis of 1956 I made a broadcast from London in a dinner jacket. It was the crown of my career until I made a broadcast in swimming trunks from the Eisenhower-Macmillan conference in Bermuda in 1957. That in turn held up until I was summoned from a tennis court when the East Germans began putting up the Berlin Wall in August, 1961. These are the things that tell you that you are important.

A similar inflation expresses itself in

the attitudes of the press toward words like sources, documents, and intelligence. Say sources and the eyes sparkle. Say documents and a hush falls. Say intelligence and people gasp in awe, as when Mephistopheles in *Faust* strikes a tavern sign and brings forth wine. Yet intelligence is only information, or misinformation. Documents are only papers, sometimes classified, or overclassified. A source is only somebody who told you something, possibly for his own purposes, and possibly incorrect.

No practice in Washington is more beloved than that of attributing statements to sources who cannot be named. It has the same appeal as secret societies with mystic rites and passwords and carries some of the same prestige a columnist acquires by referring to Gerald Ford as Gerry, Melvin Laird as Mel, Alexander Haig as Al, or the the late Charles E. Bohlen as Chip. Highly placed, or well placed, the sources may be; reliable they may be; informed, well informed, in a position to know, acquainted with the case, close to the investigation, familiar with the documents, but unnamed.

There is nothing like the Richter scale that measures earthquakes on which to rate sources; but well placed is a step below highly placed, reliable means the source has been used before, and usually reliable is a hedge. Compared to informed, well informed is slightly defensive. Acquainted with, in a position to know, close to, familiar with are only variations on informed, but may sound better in stories about trials and investigations. Authoritative is the best, since unimpeachable has been removed to another context.

There are those who prefer sources to be unnamed even though it means that those sources cannot be held responsible for what they say. It gives people in government the feeling that they are on the inside, with everybody else on the outside, and that they are among the makers and shakers in a city where competition in making and shaking is intense. Reporters enjoy the feeling that they are on the inside, too, for nothing is as valuable as an unnamed source that others cannot reach. In 1946 a member of the Anglo-American commission on Palestine told me that President Truman had privately denounced the British blockade of Palestine against ships carrying Jews. Nobody was able to match it, and nobody could knock it down because the White House would not comment. Note that even now I do not tell who the source ("a guest who sat at the President's right at the White House dinner at which he made the denunciation") was.

Using unnamed sources is often, of course, the only way information can be put out. The dogged reporting of Watergate by a small number of people demonstrated that. But it can be abused, and is too often indulged in for its own sake; and again, language is destroyed when words like reliable and sources are shrugged off and laughed at.

I have had occasion to laugh at them myself. In October, 1966, during the second of my six seasons as a play reviewer, the Broadway producer David

Merrick withdrew my first-night tickets because, he said, I was unqualified and I didn't like anything. (This is a generous way of putting it. He said I had been a washroom attendant before becoming a "Hey you, critic"; that is the head of NBC News walked into the washroom and said, "Hey you, there's a play opening tonight. Go and review it.") All this was reported at the time on radio and television, in the newspapers and in the news magazines. Later, things were patched up and my tickets were restored and NBC no longer had to pay my way into Merrick's plays.

A few years later a book called *Reviewing for the Mass Media,* whose author had asked for and received copies of some of my reviews, stated that Merrick had withdrawn my first-night tickets because I had insisted on reviewing preview performances of his productions, something I had never done with any producer. I wrote the author, who had never questioned me about the incident, telling him that he was wrong and pointing out that the facts of the incident were public knowledge at the time and getting far more attention than they were worth, which was Merrick's intention all along. The author replied that he was sorry about the mistake but he had relied on his sources.

I had visions of a clandestine phone call to the author of *Reviewing for the Mass Media,* with the source, a man of furtive movements, darting into a pay phone booth in the outer recesses of Brooklyn, identifying himself by a prearranged code, and tersely telling the phony preview story. As for why he would tell it, I supposed it must have been for the glory of being a source.

One reason that language is debased in Washington is that it rests so often on assumptions that are unexamined. As soon as a presidential election ends, it becomes the fashion to write stories and put together television programs describing the winner as close to a political genius, and finding a latent significance in every act of his childhood and early youth.

In the early and middle 1950s any British magazine editor could tell you with only a small margin of error how many copies it was worth to him to have the Queen on the cover, or the Duke of Edinburgh, or any other member of the royal family. Sensibly employed, and before satiety set in, the royal family was one of the greatest selling points the British press had. It has never entirely lost its commercial usefulness; people want to read enough about the royal family to be able to have opinions about them — that the Queen seems happy, that the Duke has made lots of changes in the palace, that poor Princess Margaret is not happy and got more than she bargained for, that Princess Anne has spirit, that Prince Charles is a quiet one but he'll come out all right. In April, 1974, a British women's magazine reminded its readers that the Queen was also a wife, a mother, and a woman with a mind of her own in an article called "The Queen the Public Doesn't Know." The subheadings were: Moved perilously close to tears; Her feet were aching so she took off her shoes; At home, she is an easy, lively conversationalist; Hurt and indignant, she asked for her coat; and It is Philip who sits at the head of the table.

Not that it is likely ever to go back to where it was at coronation time in 1953. I was riding in a bus one day along the coronation route, and men were jumping up and down on the spectators' stands that had just been erected. A little girl behind me asked her mother why the men were doing that, and the mother explained that they wanted to be sure the stands wouldn't collapse when there were people in them on Coronation Day because "That wouldn't be very nice for the Queen, would it?"

We in the American press do somewhat the same thing with our presidents and their families, especially just before and just after they take office. We are proud of them; we find qualities in them that they do not have; we want them to personify the nation, which is impossible; we write about their responsibility and opportunity to give the country moral leadership, which would be presumptuous for anybody to offer, especially somebody engaged in the day-to-day business of politics; we give the nation a fixation on them. Any journalist worth his salt writes at least a couple of articles about the new political era and new political style, and even journalists not worth their salt, though oppressed by their shortcomings, manage nonetheless. We dig up teachers who always knew that he would do great things someday. "I remember him coming to get milk and sugar for his mother," a storekeeper tells us. "He was always very careful to get the correct change. I always figured he'd make something of himself. Even then, he was all business." Quick switch to lawyer from his home town. "There was something about the way he spoke. I thought he'd become a judge for sure. Never thought he'd go into politics, though." (Chuckles.) "He seemed too serious."

A year or so after the new president has come in, two years at the most, the press discovers that he has had some failures. This makes possible another series of articles saying that the new political era may be short-lived, and that it is off to a patchy start. The press, in short, is disappointed, which it has every right to be, after taking seriously such notions as President Kennedy's Grand Design for partnership between the United States and Western Europe, the Multilateral Nuclear Force, affectionately known as the MLF, and the Alliance for Progress, also called the Alianza para el Progreso so that our neighbors to the South, who were to be transformed by it, would not feel left out. When you have an Alliance for Progress, you can count on writing articles headed The Alliance Falters quite soon.

This is not a court I enter with clean hands. I unloaded a number of stories about the Multilateral Nuclear Force and I am sure that I made loose use of Great Society and War on Poverty. It may be said that they were convenient shorthand, but there are times when that is not sufficient justification. I referred a few times to the San Antonio Formula, a proposal President Johnson put forward in San Antonio, Texas, for ending the war in Vietnam and which had not the slightest chance of doing so. I believe, however, that I never mentioned the New Frontier.

The press did it with President Johnson. He was presented as a dominating politician of near-genius, creating the Great Society in spite of other distractions. He wound up virtually a prisoner in the White House. Hubert Humphrey, as Mr. Johnson's vice-president, proclaimed that we would build the Great Society not only here but in Southeast Asia. This could have led to disappointment on a monumental scale, but it went too far. Nobody believed it.

It was done with Robert McNamara, not a president, of course, but presented as the secretary of defense with the computer brain. Computers must have data fed into them. The data are called software, a kind of mush McNamara used to ingest before he emitted the solution to whatever defense problem was bothering the country. Clicking and whirring sounds would be heard; he would look uncomfortable; and out would come a readout advocating an electronic fence along the border between the two Vietnams.

The Washington press corps, as it likes to call itself, measures happiness by the amount of its contact with the president. A failure by a president to meet the corps — a possible alternative title to "Meet the Press" — more or less regularly is seen as demeaning to the corps and, still worse, a dereliction of his duty to the American people.

I have my doubts about this, and I don't care whether the president calls me by my first name, or invites me to dinner, or telephones to congratulate me on a story, which is just as well, since all these things a succession of presidents has so far resisted the temptation to do. Information does not have to come from presidents. Can I find out what I want to find out? Is the government suppressing what should be known? These are the things that matter.

The presidential news conference is vastly overrated, anyway. This may be heresy — and I hope it is, for few things are more enjoyable than being heretical without penalty — but it would hardly matter if it weren't held at all. I am not *against* presidential news conferences if people are happy having them, and circumstances do alter cases, as they did in the Watergate summer of 1973, when we reached the stage where it was taken as an act of courage for the president of the United States to answer questions from reporters.

But no president answers anything he does not want to. It is a simple matter to say, "No comment," even though, beginning with President Kennedy's time, it seems to have been thought not sporting and shameful to do so. It is also simple to sidestep, or to drown the question rather than answer it, a technique brought to perfection by politicians on the Sunday television programs. You cannot pin down a president who does not want to be pinned down, and that is as it should be. I was bawled out by President Truman because he did not like a follow-up question I asked. He was quite right. I should not have asked it, though maybe he shouldn't have been there at a press conference to be asked it, either.

It may be argued that since those who hold news conferences choose to hold them, anything goes. We all have our fantasies:

"So, Mr. President, you thought you could get out from under with that half-baked answer. Well, you reckoned without Lank Lancelot, investigative reporter for the Honesty-Is-the-Best-Policy Syndicate."

The President tries to bluff his way out. "Listen, Lancelot, I know your kind. If you want an adversary relationship — and this goes for anybody else in this room — I can be more adversarial than you ever dreamed."

Lancelot's eyes narrow to a steely glare. "An adversary relationship is exactly what I want, Mr. President. It goes with the press card."

The President, seeing himself overmatched, tells all.

There is a cozy notion that presidential news conferences are free-swinging, no-holds-barred methods of enlightening the American people, and that they take the place of parliamentary question periods in other countries. They are not free-swinging and no-holds-barred because they cannot be, since one person at the conference is president of the United States and everbody else is not.

Nor are news conferences in any way equivalent to question periods in parliamentary countries. Those are conducted by the government and the opposition, which is an alternative government. The press is neither. Not that it might not be fun to try the parliamentary style at our news conferences. Questions are submitted in advance, "supplementaries" are allowed the questioner after the answer is given, and the Speaker may call other members who wish to ask questions:

PRESIDENT: Since I cannot accept the false premises on which the question is based, I am afraid that I am therefore unable to answer. However, I will be glad to supply detailed and factual information to show how the act cited is being carried out. (Cries of

"Hear, hear" from aides gathered behind President, and from reporters sympathetic to his point of view.)

REPORTER: Bearing in mind what the Right Honorable Gentleman has said, will he acknowledge that his administration has failed miserably in carrying out the terms of the act and that the result has been the atrociously unfair treatment of those in need? (Cries of "Hear, hear" from reporters sympathetic to Questioner's point of view.)

PRESIDENT: No sir.

SECOND REPORTER: Will my Right Honorable friend bear in mind that absurd and tendentious questions such as the one he has just been asked serve only to bring opposition parts of the press into the disrepute they so well deserve? (Cheers from President's aides and sympathetic reporters.)

PRESIDENT: I'll bear that in mind, and I thank my honorable friend.

We are told that a president must communicate with the people, that those who govern must take the people into their confidence, that there must — this is the clincher — there must be an ongoing dialogue. (It is impossible to calculate how many academic and government careers have been preserved and furthered by the devising of ongoing, or the amount of foundation money shaken loose, but that is by the way.) News conferences take care of this. So we are told.

On February 2, 1967, President Johnson held a fairly typical news conference. Would he assess the prospects for peace in Vietnam? He had said many times that we wanted a peaceful settlement and were ready for discussions, but he was not aware of any serious effort by the other side to stop the fighting. Would he be willing to take part in negotiations himself? He had no sign that the other side was willing to settle on decent terms. Would the United States compromise on its objectives? Both sides would have to make concessions, but he knew of no serious indication that the other side was ready to stop fighting. Did he note any signs of fluidity in the other side's position? He had seen no serious effort to go to the conference table or bring the war to an end.

Four questions, and essentially one answer.

Later, the President was asked what we would like from North Vietnam in exchange for stopping the bombing. He replied that he had seen no indication of reciprocal action. Still later, this question was pretty much repeated and the President pretty much repeated his answer.

Six questions, and essentially one answer.

The President was also asked about China, the new Congress, politics, Eastern Europe, and — some Washington reporters cannot resist this one — his opinion of Washington reporters (the corps!) and how he liked his job.

Presidential news conferences make news when presidents want them to, and they do not instruct presidents about what the people consider important and pressing ("the ongoing dialogue") unless presidents want them to, in which case the president probably has a shrewd idea about it all without questions from the press. Presidents don't usually think of reporters as tribunes of the people, anyway, and an ongoing dialogue would take a different form. The president begins by saying "Good evening," with 210,000,000 voices replying "Good evening" in unison, no small trick. The president announces he has good news, provoking shouts of "We'll be the judge of that" and "Let him speak." The announcement itself gets a divided reception, 42 percent in favor, 36 against, 14 don't know, and 8 don't give a damn. The president tries to reason with those who dislike his proposal; this inflames tempers further; fighting breaks out; there are occasional cries of "Thank you, Mr. President" from those who have watched too many television news conferences; the president leaves, and the ongoing dialogue ceases on to go.

Some critics of President Johnson said

that in his administration a dialogue never onwent, that he never sufficiently explained his aims and intentions in Vietnam, was not candid with the people. That was not entirely so. President Johnson communicated and communicated and communicated. He exhorted, he entreated, he adjured. He pleaded. He appealed to pride and he appealed to patriotism — March 2, 1967: "I think the American people should know that this is a question between their President, their country, their troops, and Mr. Ho Chi Minh and the troops that he is sending from the North. Everyone can take whatever side of the matter he wants to." He explained, repeatedly and at length. It is true, however, that in his administration a dialogue never onwent. A monologue onwent.

President Nixon fell into the same problem over Watergate. Every time he said something about it, his position grew worse.

There is a moral here. Communicate, by all means. But *what* is communicated may still matter. No amount of Q. and A.

can change that.

I also think it childish and time-wasting for presidents and other officials to go through "briefings" and rehearsals for news conferences in which their assistants play the parts of reporters and ask the "toughest" questions they can. It would not surprise me if reservations like those made for a popular book at a circulating library were put in early for the right to play Dan Rather, Clark Mollenhoff, and Sarah McClendon.

Here again we run into that familiar blight on public life and language, excessive calculation. Do I, then, recommend off-the-cuff answers to reporters? No. They can be too dangerous. During the Korean war, President Truman made an offhand, ambiguous answer to a question about whether consideration was being given to the use of atomic weapons. In a matter of hours the British Prime Minister, Clement Attlee, was in the air and on the way to Washington to find out what the President had meant. What he'd meant turned out to be quite different from what he'd said.

Another of Mr. Truman's offhand news conference remarks created complications of a different kind. It came during his first term, when an attorney was trying to organize a union of major league baseball players. A wartime law empowered the President to seize and operate any industry vital to national defense if its production was being interfered with, and the possibility had arisen of a strike by the Pittsburgh Pirates, the team the attorney was concentrating on. Somebody jokingly asked Mr. Truman whether he might seize them.

"I'll tell you one thing," Mr. Truman replied. "If I do, the Cardinals will have a damn good team."

When the conference ended, I was dictating a little feature about the President's remark to the United Press, for which I was then working, when one of the presidential news secretaries knocked on the door of the UP booth in the White House press room.

"Are you using the story about the

Pittsburgh Pirates?'' he asked.

I said I was.

''Don't have the President saying damn,'' he said. ''It only leads to trouble.''

The secretary meant that there would be letters, telegrams, and telephone calls to the White House about it, and maybe some petitions, and perhaps an anti-damn resolution passed here and there. So I left damn out. So did everyone else. Those were innocent days, but we shouldn't have. Also, it spoiled the story. A quarter of a century later we might have had Mr. Truman saying, ''I'll tell you one thing. If I do, the Cardinals will have a (expletive deleted) good team,'' a device that puts the burden of supplying the profanity on the reader but does nothing to reduce the no-nonsense impression the curser (or precurser, really) seeks to give.

Displays of virtuosity in answering questions may be amusing, but, though I treasure the wisecrack, I do not look to the White House for amusement. A president must be able to persuade, but if he does it better, and with less risk, in ways other than the news conference, that is his business.

In any case, it is less useful to the country to have reporters questioning a president than it is for reporters to preserve their independence. Secretary of State Dean Rusk lost his temper with some reporters about Vietnam and asked, "Which side are you on?" They were where they should have been, on the side of accurate reporting.

Secretary Rusk may well have thought theirs an "adversary relationship." It sounds persuasive, exhilarating, like a shoot-out at the O.K. Corral, and many people in government believe in it. That is no reason for the press to accept the idea. The press may be shoved into an adversary position from time to time, as it was over the Pentagon papers, but newspapers exist to print news, not to suppress it, and once they got the Pentagon papers, they had no choice, in spite of the government's attempt to enjoin publication.

It was much the same in the summer of 1973 when President Nixon, holding a news conference after going five months without one, was asked whether his authority had been eroded. He said that it had been, inevitably, because he had been attacked nightly for twelve or fifteen minutes on the news programs. The President had not been attacked; he had been reported on. These were some of the things reported:

The Watergate break-in and cover-up; the insistence by the judge in the Watergate trial on going beyond where the prosecution wanted to go; the Watergate hearings; the resistance to the idea of a special prosecutor; the unwillingness to hand over White House tapes; the break-in at the office of Daniel Ellsberg's psychiatrist; the offer of the job of FBI director to the judge in the Ellsberg case; the "enemies lists"; questionable campaign contributions; creation of the "plumbers' unit"; approval of the Huston plan, including breaking and entering, wire tapping, and mail covers; wire tapping, without court order, of a dozen journalists and White House employes; wire tapping of the

President's brother Donald; the indictment of some of the President's associates, the guilty pleas entered by others, and the resignations of still others; the disgrace and resignation of the man he twice chose for vice-president; the money spent on his houses; his tax returns; the questions raised by the ITT affair, the dairy industry affair, and the Soviet wheat deal; the pressure on corporations to contribute to his reelection campaign; the secret bombing of Cambodia and the falsification of records about it.

Walter Cronkite himself would have found his authority eroded by these things, let alone a mere president of the United States. All of this, moreover, was in addition to the firing of the special prosecutor, Archibald Cox, and the resignations of Attorney General Elliot Richardson and Deputy Attorney General William Ruckelshaus; the now-you-see-them, now-you-don't White House tapes; and the suspicions aroused by the military alert during the Middle East fighting in October, 1973.

Sometimes the President complained not that he had been attacked but that he had been subjected to a "daily pounding by the press." One of his assistants, Bruce Herschensohn, said that the President had taken a "battering" over his decision to bomb Hanoi and Haiphong in December, 1972. Vice-President Agnew had a more technical and fashionable way of putting it when he resigned. "Media interest" in his case would distract public attention from other and more important matters, Agnew said, and that was one reason he had decided to step aside. In short, it wasn't what he did but what we did, and news organizations could have chosen to cover or not to cover the case of a vice-president under grand jury investigation, as they pleased. If there had been no media interest, who knows? He might have stayed on.

Media interest appears to mean that news organizations are covering stories you don't want them to cover. This was President Kennedy's reaction — though he did not make it publicly known — when news stories began to come out of

Vietnam that showed the war ongoing not as he expected it to and, probably, not as he was being told it was. The most prominent reporter sending back not supportive but nonsupportive stories was David Halberstam of the *New York Times,* and Mr. Kennedy asked that he be replaced. The *Times* said, adversarily, no.

In an earlier intervention, Mr. Kennedy asked the *New York Times* not to print a story about the preparations being made for the Bay of Pigs invasion. The *Times* unadversarily said yes, and later Mr. Kennedy became something of a hero to parts of the press by saying that he wished the *Times* had turned him down and printed the story, because it would have saved the United States from a disaster. It was a peculiarly silly comment, since if the *Times* had printed the story, Mr. Kennedy would not have known the outcome of the invasion, and the *Times* would have been denounced for blocking an attempt to eliminate a Communist government from Cuba.

The fact is that Mr. Kennedy had quite a

different view of media interest in the days after the Bay of Pigs. I covered a speech he made at the Waldorf-Astoria in New York to a meeting of newspaper publishers. He asked them to institute a system of voluntary censorship about military matters based on the operations of the Office of War Information in the Second World War. The speech was delivered in embarrassed silence and the idea was heard of no more.

On April 1, 1968, the day after he announced that he would not run for another term, President Johnson flew to Chicago and spoke to the National Association of Broadcasters. He never quite specified his complaint, but he circled it and stalked it:

"You, the broadcasting industry, have enormous power in your hands. You have the power to clarify. And you have the power to confuse. Men in public life cannot remotely rival your opportunities because day after day, night after night, hour after hour . . . you shape the nation's dialogue.

"The commentary that you provide can

give the real meaning to the issues of the day or it can distort them beyond all meaning.''

When Mr. Johnson told the broadcasters, ''You shape the nation's dialogue,'' it was what a psychologist would call projection. ''The nation's dialogue'' was shaped by what was done in Vietnam, principally by him. Unless, of course, the news organizations had decided that a war in which 500,000 American lives were involved, which took 50,000 American lives and crippled thousands more, and cost $30,000,000,000 a year — not to mention what it did to the countries where it was fought — did not warrant media interest.

We in the news business — ''media folks,'' Mayor Richard Daley of Chicago called us in July, 1968, when he rejoiced over the prospect that a strike by electrical workers might hold up installation of communications facilities and lead to ''a good old-fashioned, old-time Democratic convention, with the delegates in charge and maybe without you media folks all over the place'' — we folks in the media interest business must be careful about what we accept. The reason is that what we accept we pass along to the nonmedia folks at home.

The war in Indochina produced a host of terms that media folks accepted at their peril: protective reaction strike, surgical bombing, free-fire zone, interdiction, contingency capability, New Life Hamlet — which in sterner days was a refugee camp — and many more. Money paid to the family of a South Vietnamese civilian killed by mistake was a condolence award.

In February, 1971, South Vietnamese ground forces, with American air support, moved into Laos. Rarely had the importance the government attached to language been made so clear. An incursion, Washington called it, and there were official objections to our calling it an invasion, evidently in the belief that incursion implied something softer than invasion did, and that an incursion was permissible where perhaps an invasion was not.

At this point, media interest led to the

dictionary, where an incursionist was defined as an invader, incursionary as invading, and incursion as entering into territory with hostile intent; a sudden invasion; a predatory or harassing inroad; a raid. The first definition of invasion mentioned conquest and plunder, and the United States was not bent on those, but the operation in Laos met other meanings of invasion precisely: an inroad of any kind, as an entry into or establishment in an area not previously occupied; the introduction or spread of something hurtful or pernicious; and a penetration or occupation by outside force or agency.

All this may be simply expressed: invasion = incursion. This being the case, why not say incursion and give the government its heart's desire? Because calling it an incursion was a public relations exercise, an attempt to make it appear less grim than it was and acceptable to the American people.

The distinction between incursion and invasion was a distinction without a difference, in grammar and in fact. The incursion into, or invasion of, Cambodia in 1970 enormously increased death and destruction there, and the incursion into, or invasion of, Laos increased death and destruction there. It is not the business of news people to exaggerate any of this, but it is not their business to water it down either.

Administrations seem to feel that he who is not in a supportive relationship with me is in an adversary relationship with me. People in the news business should turn a cold and appraising eye on all ideas, including that one. Especially that one.

A confession: I once used the word supportive while appearing on the "Dick Cavett Show." I heard it coming out and tried to pull it back. But too late. A judgment of ignominy should have been pronounced.

3

Mr. Chairman, I Find It Incumbent Upon Me

Politics has a way of bringing on meaningless language. Late in 1966, while discussing the war in Vietnam, Senator Everett Dirksen of Illinois, then the Republican leader in the Senate, reported that he heard the American people asking, "Where are we going?" just as, Dirksen said, the people of ancient Rome had asked "Quo vadis?" when Rome was nearing the end. It was a little like suggesting that the ancient Romans went around muttering "Nehercule, hoc quidem lapsus ea ruina" ("Gee whiz, this really is a decline and fall"). Dirksen probably drew his comment from a card file of appropriate reactions, under the heading Crisis Situations, or Watersheds, though the reaction was not appropriate, since it is not the Roman people but St. Peter who is usually credited with asking "Quo vadis?" and in circumstances notably different from those Dirksen set out. Still, such files are standard equipment, and few politicians are without one.

During the Republican convention in Chicago in 1960 I was walking along Michigan Boulevard when I became aware of a knot of people on the other side of the avenue. I crossed over and found Richard Nixon, then vice-president and about to be nominated for president, crouching near a shoeshine boy who was black. Crouching with him were the three Nixon women and a few cameramen.

As I arrived I heard Mr. Nixon say, "What do you want to be when you grow up?" The boy, Leon Thompson, ten years old, considered this for a while, then replied, "Well, I don't want to be no police." Mr. Nixon had a ready answer. "You don't have to be a policeman if you don't want to," he said, "In this country, you can be anything you like."

The vistas thus thrown wide, the boy considered his glowing future once more. After a while it was agreed, in the absence of other suggestions, that he would go into the army. Mr. Nixon then went on his way, and the next day NBC's "Today" show displayed its delicacy of feeling by having Leon Thompson on the program and giving him (before the cameras) a check for $200.

The politician who tries to get away from the formula reply risks creating impatience and boredom. But consider what may happen to the one who uses it. I remember Mr. Nixon representing the United States as vice-president at the independence ceremonies in Accra, Ghana, in 1957. He went to a school to announce the establishment of an Eisenhower fellowship and in the course of his speech said, "I agree with your great educator, Aggrey.* If you want to make beautiful music, you must play the black and the white notes together." As he said this, Mr. Nixon was looking out on some hundreds of black notes who were celebrating the expulsion of white notes from their country, after eighty-three years in which the black notes might almost not have been on the piano at all. The speech, probably drawn from the card file under "Negro Audiences," was not a rousing success.

There may be, nonetheless, a certain safety in language by formula, even in conversation, now that private matters have become increasingly public.

L. Patrick Gray has testified that when he called President Nixon on July 6, 1972, to tell him that some members of his staff were trying to wound him mortally, the President replied, "Pat, you just continue to conduct your thorough and aggressive investigation." This is not conclusive evidence that Mr. Nixon was speaking for

* James Emman Kwegyir Aggrey (1875 - 1927), who studied at Livingston College in Salisbury, N.C., and at Columbia University in New York.

the record, or for the recording, since he could have said, "Pat, you carry on with your thorough, aggressive, free-swinging, fearless, unremitting and let-the-chips-fall-where-they-may investigation." In any case, the President said this in San Clemente, where, so far as we know, there were no recording facilities.

However, Gray has testified that during another telephone conversation, on March 23, 1973, Mr. Nixon reminded him that he had told him to conduct a thorough investigation. Gray said this gave him "an eerie feeling," as though the President were speaking not to him but to another audience.

The White House has said that the practice of recording the President's conversations has been ended. In a way it is too bad, for conversations in which both parties, rather than only one, know they are being recorded might be models of carefully guarded talk, well worth preserving:

NIXON: Good evening, Pat.

GRAY: Good evening, Mr. President.

NIXON: What can I do for you?

GRAY: I hope this won't seem a trivial matter I've called you about.

NIXON: No need to worry. The affairs of state often weigh heavily on me — indeed, they do tonight — but I believe I must make myself available to all members of my administration for advice and counsel, if the people's interests are to be served.

GRAY: That is very good of you, Mr. President.

NIXON: Not at all. It is only what the taxpayers deserve. Now then, Pat, what is it?

GRAY: Well, Mr. President, I happened to be working late tonight — I often do — and as luck would have it a file that for months had seemed an inpenetrable mystery, and had defied my best efforts and most intense study, has at last, I have reason to believe, yielded its secret.

NIXON: I congratulate you, Pat. But are you sure that it is information that

I, even as president, should have? Is it perhaps personal in nature and therefore best kept secret, even if the interests of the nation might, at a glance and superficially considered, indicate otherwise?

GRAY: Mr. President, I put forward my own view with some hesitation, but that view is that public service often demands sacrifice, and it may compel us to engage in activities we would ordinarily find distasteful, even repellent, and which we would prefer to keep clear of. This, I believe, is such a case.

NIXON: Go on then, Pat, and you may be reassured to know that I had the FBI run a check on me after my visit to Peking. I was worried about my motives and whether I had bargained hard enough, and I thought I should be checked out. Unfortunately, with those doubts in my mind, I did not feel free to look at all the information on me that the FBI had gathered, but, on the whole, I was satisfied with my own patriotism and reliability, so I think you can go ahead.

GRAY: Mr. President, I have to inform you that a dispute has broken out in certain circles of your administration over the interpretation of your inspiring admonition, "When the going gets tough, the tough get going."

NIXON: Surely the meaning of that is beyond dispute for any real American, though I would not for one moment question the motives of anyone who did not accept that meaning, whatever the cost to the country or the additional burdens placed on me as I make the difficult decisions that peace for our children and our children's children requires.

GRAY: I quite agree, Mr. President. I had thought it not only beyond dispute but beyond cavil, as well.* Nonetheless, they have been overheard — strike that — they have been heard to say that the meaning to be drawn from the phrase depends on the interpretation of the second going. Not — if I may be allowed

* Beyond good and cavil. — Author's note.

a small joke, Mr. President — not to be confused with the Second Coming.

NIXON: Very good, Pat.

GRAY: Thank you, sir. They say that the second going can be interpreted as meaning going in a literal sense, i.e., leaving the field of battle.

NIXON: Never! Though I respect their right to an interpretation that can only help those who do not wish America well.

GRAY: Do you want a written report on this, Mr. President?

NIXON: No. I would regard that as an unjustifiable invasion of privacy. I think this calls for a directive, but naming no names. Perhaps I can write it this weekend. No rest for the weary, eh, Pat?

GRAY: Exactly, Mr. President. Thank you, Mr. President.

Still, there is no need to invent language for those in Washington. The real thing serves very well:

"I am considering offering my capacity for state-wide leadership."

Representative Hugh Carey of New York, on being asked whether he would run for the Democratic nomination for governor in 1974.

"No serious thought [of the nomination] will be permitted in my mind while I am undertaking the most painful duty of my political career." Senator Howard Baker of Tennessee, on being asked whether he would try for the Republican presidential nomination in 1976.

"I believe the present situation clearly indicates that in the second quarter we're going to be in a posture where gas rationing may well be a reality." Senator Henry Jackson, Democrat of Washington, speaking about the gasoline situation after three days of hearings in January, 1974.

"At once original, bold, comprehensive, measured and timely." James Lynn, Secretary of Housing and Urban Development, commenting on President Nixon's housing message of 1973.

The above is a fair sampling of Washington language, spoken by those who seek to show themselves worthy of larger responsibilities, who solemnly demonstrate that they put the nation's interest before their own, and who sternly, uncompromisingly, and ambiguously face facts.

Lynn's dutiful hyperbole sounded as though it came from his department's public relations machine. Very likely it did. Much of the language in Washington is produced by speech writers, and while some of them are clever, speech writers are bad for language.

There undoubtedly are politicians who, nine months old and about to move from breast to bottle, thanked their mothers for making the determination that they should be weaned and for nourishment that had been comprehensive, measured, and timely. They can make stilted speeches without help. I have been told, too, that an actor may come to feel that the words the playwright gave him are his own. Politicians probably do the same with the words cranked out for them, and once they speak the words, the responsibility is theirs. But when speech writers are used, what is personal to the speaker is minimized, whereas when a politician uses his own words, they tell us something about the speaker. William Simon, when he was head of the Federal Energy Office, replied, "That would be judgmental," when asked when gasoline rationing might begin if it were ordered. In an earlier era the equivalent answer would have been, "That's an iffy question." Iffy is coy but people who used it merely thought they were clever. People who say judgmental think they are important.

In any case, we in the news business are being unfair to writers, and inaccurate as well. For years we should have been reporting, "President Kennedy, in a speech largely written by Theodore Sorenson and Arthur Schlesinger, Jr., said today . . ." and "President Nixon, using words and ideas principally supplied by Patrick Buchanan, said today . . ." On January 16, 1974, we should have reported, "Vice-President Ford today attacked George Meany, president of the AFL-CIO, Americans for Democratic Action, and other 'pressure organizations' calling for the impeachment of President Nixon. The original draft of Ford's speech was prepared by writers in the White House."

Ford explained later that he had had to use White House speech writers because his own staff was still in process of formation and he could not call on writers of his own. He also said that the original draft had been prepared from ideas he supplied. That may have been Ford's pride speaking, but suppose Ford had not supplied the ideas? Suppose the White House led him to make the first bellicose speech of his vice-presidency, thereby antagonizing some of those who wanted him to replace President Nixon as soon as possible, and so strengthening Mr. Nixon's grip on the White House? Ford made the speech. The responsibility for it would still have been his.

I do not, however, withdraw my statement that we in the news business are being unfair and inaccurate when we do not say who the writers of a particular speech are. Writers are identified at the end of television programs. Maybe they should be identified at the end of political speeches. The term used for the list of names given at the end of television programs is credits. That takes a lot for granted, but the practice is sound.

If the speech writer is an enemy of language because he conceals, or in some cases distorts, the politician's personality and talent, so is the public opinion poll, for it also depersonalizes, and anything that depersonalizes is an enemy of language. The poll has a deadening effect on politics, and its effect on language is an extension of that. It encourages predictability, and it encourages the tailoring of positions, and so of language, to whatever the poll indicates is desirable.

I am reminded of something that happened in January, 1972, when, God help us, ten months before the election, campaigning in the New Hampshire primary was about to begin. There were many new voters in New Hampshire that year — either young people newly enfranchised or people who had moved in from other states — and so somebody associated with Senator Edmund Muskie was quoted as saying, "The big problem is that we know virtually nothing about these voters," while associates of Senator George McGovern were devising a questionnaire to find out who the new voters were and what was on their minds.

This was an interesting case of getting things backward. True, the new voters had not been questioned in depth, height, and width about their political positions, and some had even crossed state lines in that depraved condition. But politicians don't have to know who the voters are. Voters have to know who the politicians are. Any politician will want to know what people are concerned about. That is part of the job, and, beyond that, nobody running for office does it for the exercise. It is too expensive and demanding for that.

But the minute examination of the electorate has become depressingly familiar — the polling and the cross-polling, the calculation of how to make the appeal that is most productive in votes. Polling has become a malign influence on our politics. It may distort the political process by contributing to a band-wagon effect, by creating impressions that handicap candidates, and even by destroying candidates before they begin campaigning in earnest. A defeat may be softened because the loser got more votes than the polls indicated he would. A victory in a primary may be made equivocal, or turned into a defeat, because the victor did not get as large a margin as the polls said he would.

Muskie was an example. He became known as a man who had a big lead and lost it. On primary night in New Hampshire you could hear it said over and over again that Muskie went into New Hampshire two months before with a commanding 65 percent of the vote. His primary percentage — 48 percent — was compared with that, to his disadvantage. For Muskie, it was the beginning of the end. Ask not for whom the public opinion polls; it polls for thee.

But did Muskie go into New Hampshire with a commanding 65 percent of the vote? There was a poll that said so, but even if it was accurate, it was irrelevant. Elections are held when they are held, not before, and not after.

The poll has the same appeal that other social science jargon has, but there is no evidence that opinion polling in advance of an election in any way improves the governing process. When the polls miss, the usual explanation is that they neglected to poll right up to the last minute, which happens to be election time anyway, or that they always said they operated within a 3 percent margin of error, which happens to be enough to decide many elections. Another justification is that they are meant to be a "useful tool" and no more. What is their usefulness? Even when the polls turn out to be accurate forecasts of what is to come, what is to come still has to come. We might as well wait for it.

If politicians want to use polls, nothing can stop them. Indeed, if news organizations want to use polls, nothing can stop them either, and nothing has. They get deeper into polling with each election. But it is a bad business, because it puts the emphasis in an election in the wrong place, on who is thought to be ahead, rather than on what the candidates propose and what their election might mean.

I never mention polls except to deprecate them. On election night anyone with that attitude could easily feel like Edmond Dantes in the Château d'If. However, with me, it appears to be considered only an eccentricity that comes with age, and in any event nobody is distracted from coverage of that momentous question: Were the polls right?

Politicians should be encouraged to stand for what they believe in, not to try to smell out the exact mosaic of attitudes and positions that will appeal to the greatest number. Politicians should also be responsive to the popular will. But if the popular will does not coincide with his own, each politician has to work that out with his own conscience, and the voters must decide how far they want their representatives to mirror them and their feelings. Government by poll, which is to say by statistical sample, is uninspiring and distressing.

Finally — and here is where the effect

of polls on language is so profound —
because they help to set a style of
expression, public opinion polls have
become one of the great institutional
bores of our time. Ask not on whom the
public opinion palls; it palls on me. In 1968
a Lou Harris poll on Hubert Humphrey
showed that a majority of those
questioned thought Humphrey was long-
winded. What a revelation!

At a recent British by-election, a
victorious candidate, a Scottish
Nationalist, was interviewed by the BBC.
The interviewer, bemused by polls,
projections, swings, and other esoterica,
asked: Would you say that the result was
a success for you?

CANDIDATE: I won the seat, if that
is what you mean by success.

I said earlier that anything that
depersonalizes is an enemy of language
and that the poll does depersonalize. It
reached its logical conclusion — I *hope* it
is the conclusion — in a study of voters'
reactions to televised political advertising

in the Nixon-McGovern campaign for the Citizens Research Foundation of Princeton, New Jersey. The authors, Thomas E. Patterson and Robert D. McClure, explained that their research was "rooted in a specific psychological theory of attitude organization and change — the attitude-belief model developed by Martin Fishbein. In operationalizing the Fishbein model," they went on, "measures of the following variables were obtained during each personal interview wave: issue and candidate image attitudes, beliefs about candidates' issue positions and image characteristics, salience of issues and images, and beliefs about the salience of issues and images to the candidates."

After operationalizing the Fishbein model, Patterson and McClure concluded: "We have a rather precise standard for judging the effectiveness of persuasive political messages. If a campaign communication has a positive effect, more voters will change their attitude-belief relationship in a favorable direction between one time and a later time [i.e.,

$p(a_ib_iC(t)<a_ib_iC(t+1))]$ than will change their attitude-belief relationship in an unfavorable direction $[p(a_ib_iC(t) > a_ib_iC(t+1))]$."

The finding that an effective message wins over more voters $[p(a_ib_iC(t) < a_ib_iC(t+1))]$ than it loses $[p(a_ib_iC(t) > a_ib_iC(t+1))]$ must have stirred politicians all over the country. The use of the term interview wave unquestionably did the same for social scientists.

In addition to the damage the poll does to language, it discourages spontaneity and aggrandizes the predictable, whereas life is more fun when not everything can be foreseen. In the 1930s there was a Greta Garbo movie called *Queen Christina*. In it she played a seventeenth-century Queen of Sweden who liked to go out among the people, disguised as a young man, to see how the common folk were faring. One day she rode too far and had to stay overnight at an inn.

Along came the new Russian ambassador, played by John Gilbert, en route to the royal court at Stockholm, where he was to take up his post. He could not make Stockholm by nightfall, so he also stopped at the inn. Because the inn was crowded, the landlord told him that he would have to put him in a room that had only a double bed, which he would have to share with a young man. Did he mind?

The ambassador said he did not mind, and went up to the room occupied by Greta Garbo.

''Sorry about this,'' said the ambassador, ''but this is the only thing they had available.''

''That's all right,'' said Greta Garbo in her deepest and manliest voice.

''I'm tired,'' said the ambassador. ''Think I'll turn in.''

''Yeah, me too,'' said Greta Garbo, and took off her jacket, whereupon the ambassador, who happened to be looking in her direction, said, ''Life is so gloriously unpredictable.''

In those days, there were no polls.

There were no elections either, of course. I do not presume to say whether that was good or bad, but it did have this to be said for it: there was at least no ethnic approach to the electorate.

Here is a candidate for mayor of New York kicking off his campaign. His name is John Marchi and he is a Republican member of the State Senate. A television reporter approaches, places himself in front of his station's camera, and notes that it is raining as Marchi's campaign begins. "Does that have any meaning for you, Senator?" he asks.

Marchi does restrain himself. He does not say, "Itsa rain. Thatsa good." All the same, a large, dutiful smile spreads across his face. "My people believe it means good luck," he replies.

That's a good reason to vote for a man.

The ethnic approach is not confined to politics. Excerpt from a letter sent out by the American Jewish Committee:

"Dear Friend:

"The energy crisis obviously confronts all of us as American citizens, and raises particular intergroup and interreligious questions of concern to the Jewish and Christian communities."

Probably what they wanted to head off was Jews getting gasoline on even-numbered days and Christians getting gasoline on odd-numbered days. It could have led to bad feelings, or, to use the technical term, divisiveness.

The tribal attitude did not come about because of the sheer perversity of immigrants and their offspring. There were many causes. Banding together within immigrant groups for protection, mutual help, and understanding has always been a factor in American life, and after the Second World War new forces pushed in the same direction. The countries of Western Europe recovered economically and politically, and Americans went to live in them, and there came to be no opprobrium involved in being associated with them. Many foreign products proved to be superior to their American counterparts and better adapted to American life, and with that foreign products took on a certain glamor (though it helped to sell them if they were called imported rather than foreign).

These developments coincided with the decline of the American city, which took some of the shine off the American dream, and with the war in Vietnam, which weakened the central loyalty of Americans to their country and led some of them to search for loyalties that were more immediate and closer to home. The ethnic connection lay to hand. Finally, there was the black revolt, an outburst that convinced other groups that they and their grievances were being overlooked and led them to use the same tactics.

So it happened that Eugene McCarthy, in his book *The Year of the People,* recalled hearing in the spring of 1968 that Robert Kennedy's organization had set up twenty-six committees to deal with twenty-six different kinds of Americans. McCarthy remarked at the time that he had heard of twenty-six different flavors of ice cream, but he had not know there were that many kinds of Americans.

So it happened also that President Nixon said that he was pleased to have Vice-President Agnew, with his Greek background, in his administration. This statement was made early in Mr. Nixon's first term. Later, Mr. Nixon was pleased to have Agnew, with his Greek background, out of his administration. But the point remains that it was a doubtful kind of appeal to make. True, Mr. Nixon was speaking to the Ethnic Groups Division of the Republican National Committee, which tries to offset Democratic pioneering in this area, but suppose Agnew were of Russian, or Scandinavian, or Polynesian background? What difference would it make? Mr. Nixon's own ancestry is Scottish and Irish. Should we be writing stories that begin, "President Nixon, who is of Scottish and Irish ancestry, today signed a bill authorizing the modernization of seven bankrupt railroads in the Northeast and Middle West"?

Agnew himself spoke to the Ethnic Groups Division of the Republican National Committee after Mr. Nixon did, and said that his background actually was Greek and English, thereby setting off a thrill of pleasure felt as far away as London, Manchester, and Leighton Buzzard, Bedfordshire. Agnew remarked also that his wife was of German, Irish, English, and French extraction, thereby making her an ideal politician's wife.

After Agnew was forced to resign, an NBC elevator operator said to me, "Well, I guess we Greeks won't be getting any more big jobs for a while." At about the same time another NBC employe explained that she had a vivid imagination because she was a Hungarian.

I suppose one should know these things about oneself, or cannot help knowing them, but what is the point? I find all this so depressing that I think we should change the election date in New York City so that the campaign never again coincides with religious holidays. In November, 1969, the contest for mayor became a contest over which candidate could wear his skull cap into more synagogues than the others. Prime Minister Golda Meir of Israel visited New York during the campaign, and Mayor John Lindsay, running for reelection and afraid he had lost the "Jewish vote" because of what some considered his excessive solicitousness about blacks, barely stopped short of proposing marriage to her.

A catalogue of ethnic stalking of public office in New York City alone would run into volumes, extending far beyond the well-known indigestion tour of pizza, Chinese egg rolls, and the like. In 1961 a candidate for president of the City Council sent out campaign literature printed in green ink, with a map of Ireland as the background and the counties of Kerry and Cork marked in. That's a good reason to vote for a man.

I know there are large numbers of people who do not agree with me about this. The idea of group rights, as distinct from individual rights, is spreading. As might have been predicted, it has been legitimized and given an imposing name — pluralism, the pluralistic society. There is much in it that is logical and understandable. If you are a member of a group that has been rejected, or at any rate not favored, it is natural to respond by insisting that the group is good, and then you take pride in it, and then you make a virtue of necessity and argue that clannishness is a good thing in itself.

It is understandable, and it is not for me

to tell people who have suffered because of their name or skin color how they should react. Those groups are entitled to use place of origin and skin color in their own interest, as such personal characteristics have been used against their interest, but I cannot see that it makes any sense to encourage the ethnic outlook. It bases policies and attitudes on considerations that should be irrelevant.

Pluralism is, of course, the kind of word social scientists love, though it is giving way with surprising speed to a new entry, multi-ethnic, and the hyphenated American approach to politics is growing stronger as a result of its acceptance not only among politicians but among social scientists, who appear to welcome the fact that we are not becoming the single, integrated, melting-pot society that was envisaged for so long, and to revel in it because it gives them such good material. It also fattens the social scientific vocabulary. The pluralistic ideal becomes creative ethnicity, defined as ethnic groups learning about themselves and one another in order to interact constructively.

I am made uncomfortable when I hear the breakdown of voting results according to religion and race and national origin. Not because it is not a generally efficacious way to figure out how an election is going — its efficacy has been demonstrated — but because it helps to perpetuate divisions that we might be better off without, because it leads people to go on thinking of themselves in a particular way, as members of a particular group, which may have little connection with the issues the election is about.

I have another reason that seems to have been generally overlooked, which is that this exhaustive research, this pinpointing classification, tends to destroy the privacy and secrecy of the voting booth. You do not know how an individual votes, but you do know how an individual is likely to vote, because you do know how the group of which he is, electronic data procedurally speaking, a member is likely to vote. Still more, he knows how he is expected to vote. The consequence of that, it seems to me, is the promotion of excessive calculation among politicians. I think we are better off when we calculate less.

We in the news business contribute to this by the way we break down and analyze the votes. We talk about the black vote and the Jewish vote and the Italian vote, and where they've gone and who got them. We discover a trend among unfrocked Catholic priests in northern Rhode Island, and there is no holding us. It takes some work to do this, and it costs a lot of money, and I have been thinking that it might be done more simply and at less cost. When people register to vote, they could indicate whether they intend to cast a Serbo-Croat vote, or a Coptic Christian vote, or whatever it may be. That would be entered on their registration card, and when they entered the polling place on election day they could be directed to an appropriate machine — a machine for Seventh-Day Adventist votes only, for example — and we could have our analysis ready much sooner.

This may sound like know-nothingism, and standing in the way of the social sciences, and opposing the advance of knowledge, but I don't think it is. Multiethnicity is much more attractive to those who are not mono-ethnic themselves, and pluralism is more comfortable for those who are on the inside than it is for those who are out. As for opposing the advance of knowledge, anybody who has ever done graduate work knows that a vast amount of pointless information is collected by academics. I do not say that they should not collect this information if they want to. I do say that it is part of an unfortunate and damaging preoccupation, and calling the society multi-ethnic does not change that.

That same preoccupation may be seen in that bit of charmless Americana, "the Polish joke," and now that a few million dollars a year have become available under the federal Ethnic Heritage Studies Act, I suppose we may look forward to doctoral theses on the subject: "The Polish Joke: Multiple Manifestations of Interpersonal and Intergroup Stress in a

Pluralistic Society, 1962 - 63."

I went on the "Today" show one morning to say that I was tired of ethnic jokes and would like to hear no more of them. I mentioned Polish jokes, among others. Letters came in praising me for "sticking up for the Poles," and I was asked to go on again to tell about the record of Polish Americans in Pennsylvania in volunteering for military service in the Second World War. Since I had said that all that Polish jokes amounted to was that Poles were stupid, I was also accused of saying that Poles were stupid. So much for the influence of the electronic medium in shaping the nation's dialogue.

I am not suggesting that American humor be denatured, that the vigor and bite be taken out of it. I know that much of the humor in this country, for as long as anyone now alive can remember, has been ethnic. That was logical and unavoidable: the unintentional misuse of English by immigrants who understood it imperfectly often had amusing results. The difficulty that many of the newcomers had in adapting to the customs of the United States also gave rise to amusing situations, though these often had overtones of sadness as well.

The result was a robust kind of humor, sometimes endearing, sometimes cruel, but one that many people could recognize as having some application to themselves. Even today, some ethnic content in American humor is still inevitable. But the Polish and Italian and Hungarian jokes we have been hearing for so long are manufactured and mechanical and boring to a lot of us. They have been persisted in for so long that they have taken on a meanness of spirit. They appear to be substitutes for the jokes about "niggers" that are, happily, no longer heard in public. One is driven to suspect that many of those who so airily toss off the Polish jokes and the rest really believe them. It is not a laughing matter.

I think, as I said, that we are better off when we calculate less, but politicians (and who can blame them? See how British Prime Minister Edward Heath became just British Edward Heath when

166

he impetuously called a general election at the end of February, 1974, sixteen months before he had to?) do not appreciate the glorious uncertainties of life. By and large they prefer the controlled and dependable. Spontaneity is all right, provided they can rehearse it first.

I am reminded of an incident involving a United States senator. It would be unfair to say who he is, because his notes were for himself and I saw them only because we were seated next to each other in such a way that it was impossible for me not to see them. He was on "Meet the Press" at a time when he had some hope of being nominated for president. Accordingly, he found it necessary to give himself some advice and to keep that advice before him. He therefore listed these reminders:

"1. Candid. Straightforward.
"2. Thoughtful.
"3. Modest.
"4. Some very short answers."

Finally, if he should be asked about the political significance of the defeat of Governor Ronald Reagan's proposal to limit personal income taxes in California, the answer he suggested to himself, in case it should otherwise slip his mind, was

"5. I don't know."

There is something dispiriting in the knowledge that politicians have to remind themselves to be candid. Also, I suppose the adjuration regarding thoughtfulness was less to be thoughtful than to appear it. But for modesty, the admission of ignorance, and, still more, very short answers, we can only be grateful.

I would not, of course, claim that a politician's language will always be more engaging if it is his own and spontaneous.

The following glittering performance opened the "Meet the Press" program of Sunday, August 16, 1964. I was the moderator, and Lawrence Spivak was questioning Robert Wagner, then mayor of New York:

MR. SPIVAK: Mayor Wagner, Attorney General Kennedy said the other day, and I quote, "Under no circumstances would I ever have considered or would I now consider coming into the State of New York against the wishes of the Mayor."

If he seeks the Senate seat from New York, will it be against your wishes?

MAYOR WAGNER: I saw the Attorney General a week ago Friday and discussed generally the matter with him, and at that time he said that he would want to think it over a bit more to decide whether he would like to come in and seek the Democratic nomination for Senator, and we both agreed that, given that opportunity to think it over — and I would also have the opportunity to canvass a bit and discuss the matter with various people and those who have various political leanings within the Democratic Party — I will see the Attorney General in the next day or so and find what he has in mind also at that time explore the possibilities with him.

I may say that there has been a certain amount of criticism of his candidacy. There has also been a good support among various factions. I emphasized, too, with him, that I felt to come in under the original support that he had, which he said was no part of his understanding in the matter, of some of the so-called political bosses was not the best way to come in.

MR. SPIVAK: Mr. Mayor, that is all very interesting, but the question was, if he seeks the Senate seat from New York, will it be against your wishes?

MAYOR WAGNER: I think I could better answer that, Mr. Spivak, after I have had an opportunity to talk to him and we, number one, find out whether he is interested, and then talk about some matters to make sure that, if he would be in, it would not in any way prevent what we have tried to do, and that is, make the Democratic Party a little more representative of the rank and file.

MR. SPIVAK: Are you saying that as

of now you are neither for nor against him?

MAYOR WAGNER: True.

MR. SPIVAK: Certainly you have given a great deal of thought to the subject.

MAYOR WAGNER: That is true. I would be able to answer that question as to whether I would approve of his coming in after I have had a further talk with him.

MR. SPIVAK: Is there much question in your mind — there isn't in the minds of many other political observers — but that he would like to come into New York, would like to run for the Senate?

MAYOR WAGNER: I must say that since I have last talked to him, he has been away. There have been a lot of people apparently talking about this matter. I don't know whether they truly represent his thinking. I find oftentimes — I read about "sources close to City Hall," "spokesmen for the Mayor say this," when I have never said any such thing, and I would rather hear it from the individual concerned, directly.

MR. SPIVAK: We would like very much to hear it directly from you, too, Mr. Mayor.

MAYOR WAGNER: I am sure we will give it directly to you after I have had the opportunity to see him in the next day or so.

MR. SPIVAK: Almost everyone else has given us your reasons for refusing to endorse him, because that is exactly what you have done to date: you have refused to endorse him. Will you give us your reasons now, your own reason directly for refusing to endorse him, because evidently you have many restrictions in your mind about endorsing him, or you would have come right out for him?

MAYOR WAGNER: First of all, I think we should know whether he is a candidate or not. I think that is important, because if he is not a candidate then the party must seek another person as a candidate or find out whether he is in the field with those candidates who have already announced or are available.

Secondly, I want to clear up this point, that I have never opposed Mr. Kennedy's coming into this race because of any fear that he would then share in the power or take over the Democratic Party in the State of New York. I have never felt that way. I would like to have more people interested in running for high office here, more people who have ability to be available for important positions in the party, and I have never felt that I would be opposed to anyone running for the Senate because they might in any way interfere with my political position because —

MR. SPIVAK: You have admitted very little in answer to my questions, but will you admit this, that if he does come in, there is a chance that you may oppose him?

MAYOR WAGNER: I would say that if he comes in, I think he would come in under circumstances that would be best for him and also good for the party.

Even this verbatim account does not give the true flavor of the exchange, because Wagner dropped innumerable "ahs" into his replies and slowed them still more, and these were thoughtfully excised by the monitoring service. When Spivak sank back, exhausted, and we went into a commercial break, Wagner, exhilarated, turned to me.

"I love this fencing," he said.

Wagner is a Democrat. We have a two-party system, however. Not to be outdone:

December 11, 1973. The Red Room of the State Capitol, Albany, New York. Governor Nelson Rockefeller:

"I will resign next Tuesday after fifteen years of service to the people of the state.

"... after long and careful consideration, I have concluded that I can render a greater public service to the people of New York and the nation by devoting myself to the work of two bypartisan national commissions ...

"Because I feel this so deeply, I'm resigning as governor in order to be able to devote my energies to the success of these commissions. My only regret is that my undertaking these tasks has been interpreted as a political maneuver to seek the Presidency . . .

". . . above all, my deep gratitude to the people of New York State as a whole. By electing me four times as your governor you granted me a unique opportunity of public service. I thank you for this privilege."

According to the Citizens Research Foundation, Rockefeller and his family put up more money than any American had ever spent before to obtain public office. The Foundation calculated that Rockefeller's campaign spending from 1952 to 1970, while he ran for governor four times and for the Republican presidential nomination three times, exceeded $27,000,000. In Rockefeller's 1970 campaign alone, the Citizens Research Foundation said, $4,500,000 came from his family. His stepmother gave $2,803,500; his brothers and sister gave $1,448,533 altogether. More than $7,700,000 was spent in 1970, almost as much as by the state's other candidates for governor and its candidates for United States senator combined. This kind of thing tends to make the people's grant of unique opportunities for public service more likely.

Still, Rockefeller nearly convinced me that he was giving up his presidential ambitions. He did that with the reference at the beginning of his remarks to "long and careful consideration." Men interested in being president usually give "long and prayerful consideration."

Further, it appeared that Rockefeller would fail to speak of the people's hopes and aspirations, not what one would expect from a man with an eye on 1976. He caught himself in time, however. "No one is more aware of the people in all areas of this state, their hopes and aspirations, as well as their concerns," he said. True, he was speaking of his successor, Malcolm Wilson, but the requisite words were there.

Wilson, lieutenant governor for fifteen years, was ready:

"Your historic announcement today will soon place the executive leadership of the state on my shoulders. And with God's help, my total commitment will be to give the best within me to the responsibilities of that high office.

"Fortunately your decision is not to withdraw from public service but rather, as a private citizen, to devote your vast experience, your deep knowledge, your great courage, your total integrity, and your compassionate concern for all people to the critical issues which challenge all America.

"I know, Nelson, that I reflect the sentiments of all New Yorkers when I say that we receive your decision with profound emotion, with regret certainly, for your having given us fifteen years of achievement unparalleled by any governor in this nation's history."

The language of Rockefeller and Wilson on that cold December morning in Albany was wasted on an off year in a state capital. It belonged at a party nominating convention. That is where fulsome political language goes unbridled and unabashed. It can be frightful to listen to, for politicians still exist who will look out upon an audience and say that they would rather live in a modest cottage, surrounded by books, family, and friends, than occupy the most splendid post ever conceived by the mind of man, after which they would rather lie in the corner of a tiny country churchyard than in the tombs of the Capulets. In the meantime, they may sacrifice every other personal consideration in the quest for office, and lie, cheat, and steal in the pursuit of power, but the language is marvelous, and it is in place.

It was in the middle of August, 1972, only a week before it was to begin, that it came home to me that the Republicans were going to hold a convention. The confirmation came when a man addressing the Republican National Committee spoke of ''these United States.'' You can go for four years without hearing that, and with the country known as it usually is — the United States. Come the conventions and ''these United States'' pops out once more.

It is a heavily laden political phrase. It makes its bow to state feelings, and conventions are organized by states and presidential elections decided by the electoral votes of states. It has a special appeal to states' rights people and has, over the years, charmed the South.

The oratorical flourish does not stop there. Individual states are often referred to as sovereign, which they are not, since they do not have armed forces and do not conduct foreign policy, two irreducible attributes of sovereignty. But it is a ringing word, sovereign, and it is stored away with "these United States" until the conventions make it legitimate to use it once more.

Conventions have a language of their own. They also have an atmosphere, a manner, which is less easy to define than to describe, though heavy-handed humor is one of its unfailing characteristics. At the Republican convention in Chicago in 1960, Wendell Corey, the master of ceremonies, began with a request to clear the aisles, followed by this: "Please, let's not look like a bunch of Democrats in Los Angeles." The hall echoed with laughter and applause, and the aisles were cleared.

A bit later on came another joke, this one from the national committeewoman from Illinois, Mrs. C. Wayland Brooks, about how before the Democratic convention in Los Angeles, Chicago had been thought to be the world's windiest city, but now Los Angeles was.

This did not compare unfavorably with a joke told at the Democratic convention by Senator Sam Ervin of North Carolina, long before his Watergate days: "I have a grandson who is four years old. In December, my little grandson came to my house on Sunday to have dinner with his grandparents and one of the neighbors was there, and the neighbor said to my little grandson, 'Jimmy, did you go to Sunday School this morning?' He said, 'Yes, I went to Presbyterian Sunday School.' The neighbor said, 'Jimmy are you a Presbyterian?' Jimmy said, 'No, I am a Democrat.'"

Convention language as such begins to be heard before the daily session officially opens, when the delegates who arrive early are entertained. Thus, at the Republican convention in San Francisco in 1964, the actor Victor Jory: "We are proud to present a worthy representative of our own very wonderful Republican women, a very special combination, I might add, an active party official who also has a beautiful singing voice, Mrs. Trefinna R. Wilson, who is the Republican committeewoman of the Fifth District of the Second Ward of the city of Wilmington, Delaware, a wonderful contralto."

I don't remember how well Mrs. Wilson sang, but Jory's performance was wonderful, which is to say routine.

In any convention, the adjective heard most often is great. If entertainers are provided, they may be described as wonderful, even if nobody listens to them, which is usually what happens.* Everything else is great. If a wonderful entertainer is to sing "O Sole Mio," it is a great song, and the wonderful entertainer gives a great performance. If a display of great friendship kindles a glow in somebody's heart, it is a great glow. The

* See case of Mrs. Trefinna R. Wilson, *supra.*

convention is a great gathering.

Even the clergymen who pray at the beginning and end of each session are great. On the second day of the Democratic convention of 1968, Senator Daniel Inouye of Hawaii introduced Billy Graham:

"It is my privilege and honor* to call upon a great American, a great theologian, a great religious leader, to invoke the divine blessings."

No politician will put in an appearance without being heralded as great, and those of middle age and older have a better than even chance of being called statesmen as well. And anybody who presents anybody else to the convention will be overwhelmed by his great good fortune in doing so. The ideal introduction was delivered in 1960 by the Democratic national chairman, Paul Butler, for the keynote speaker, Senator Frank Church of Idaho. Butler had a great pleasure and privilege, plus great pleasure and personal pride, in presenting a great

* Privilege and honor go together at conventions.

American who was a great, able, and outstanding member of a great deliberative body.

In 1968, at Miami Beach, after the mayor, Jay Dermer, had somewhat puzzlingly announced that he was there to "extend our heart and our heartbeat" to the delegates, the Republicans had a bout of baton passing. Senator George Murphy of California introduced from "the great state of Tennessee" Senator Howard Baker, who introduced "one of America's greatest public servants," Senator Edward Brooke of Massachusetts, who presented from the "the great state of Wyoming" Senator Clifford Hansen, who introduced to "the great convention of 1968" from "the great state of Oregon" Senator Mark Hatfield, for whom it was "a great pleasure" to introduce "a great person," Senator Charles Percy of Illinois, who introduced from "the great middle-western state of Michigan" Senator Robert Griffin, who being last had nobody to introduce and remained silent.

At the Republican convention in

Chicago in 1960 it fell to Mayor Daley, who though a Democrat was the host mayor, to make it clear at the outset that great would not be slighted and tradition would be upheld. Daley therefore referred to the great city, that being Chicago; the great year, that being 1960, the only year available to him at the time; the great convention city, again Chicago; our great country; the great convention, that being the one that nominated Abraham Lincoln a hundred years earlier; a great country, the United States; these great centers, the local urban communities; the great central cities of our nation, which include Chicago; our great beach, the beach of Lake Michigan; and a great people, this being the American people.

This great speech by Chicago's great mayor lasted two minutes and drew great applause.

In 1968 Daley was addressing his own party, but it made no noticeable difference. He spoke of the Democrats' great chairman, John Bailey of Connecticut; Illinois's great governor, Samuel Shapiro; and the great political gathering that was taking place in one of the greatest neighborhoods of Chicago — his.

He pointed out that Americans had created more great cities than any nation in history, that 1968 was a great time of change, that the United States was a great country, that Chicago was a great city, that Chicago was one of the greatest cities in the world, that it was a great convention, and that the United States was a great country.

Shapiro followed. He told the delegates that Chicago was a great city. He mentioned Illinois's tradition of having great governors, described the Democrats as the greatest force for unity in America and the greatest force for progress, order, and justice, called the United States the greatest nation in the history of the world, and ventured the prediction that men the convention nominated would be great Democrats.

Soon after Mayor Daley's 1960 speech, Senator Karl Mundt of South Dakota presented a gavel to the convention chairman, Senator Thruston Morton of

Kentucky. Mundt inexplicably missed the opportunity to call it a great gavel, but he recovered and pointed out that it had been made by a professor at South Dakota's great agricultural college. Mundt then demonstrated how dangerous it is for convention speakers to leave the well-trodden ways. He told Morton that the gavel was massive in size, although massive does not describe size but solidity of composition, and that it was made of endurable maple, although maple furniture, while popular, is not everyone's favorite, and it was surely for Senator Morton to say whether he wished to endure it.

Gavels have a special place at conventions. They exemplify the core of cliché and sentiment. I have seen one presented to a convention chairman that was made from the tongue of a covered wagon, and another made from a purple beech tree planted at Monticello by Thomas Jefferson. The Virginia delegate who handed over the purple beech gavel said he hoped it would sound as a claxon. The trick with gavels is to make them from great and important pieces of wood, and unless Mount Vernon becomes available for the purpose, Monticello will clearly hold pride of place. At Chicago in 1968, Liv Bjorlie, national committeewoman for North Dakota, gave John Bailey a gavel made from timber removed from the Monticello mansion during its renovation in 1954. "This gavel," Mrs. Bjorlie said, "represents the foundation of our democracy." Bailey banged it on the table and pronounced it good.

At the Republican convention in 1968, local boosterism crept in. Three orangewood gavels were presented, to the temporary chairman, the permanent chairman, and the chairman of the Republican National Committee. In their acknowledgments they spoke of the great state of Florida (twice), the great orange industry (twice), and the great convention (twice), also known as the great event (once).

To conclude our consideration of great: Much time and effort could be saved if great were understood to occur before each noun to which it might conceivably apply. At conventions, to call something great is to damn it with faint praise, rather like the routine description of each candidate for the nomination as the next president of the United States.

In 1968 Gerald Ford sensed this. Montana, he said, was "one of our very great, great Western states."

Skipping lightly over the formal speeches and debates on the party platforms (though this slights such statements as that by John Bailey in 1968 when, almost visibly pulling himself together, he asserted his long devotion to the party by saying, "In convention assembled, I cast my vote for Roosevelt, Truman, Stevenson, Kennedy, and Johnson"; and by Catherine Peden of Kentucky in the same hall, "If we are to continue as the party of hope, we must refuse to play patty-cake opportunism"; and by Elly Peterson of Michigan to the Republicans in 1964, when she said, "I hold no brief for power-hungry politicians who would nibble away at our freedom," without telling why politicians hungry for power should be eating freedom instead; and by Lieutenant Governor Jared Maddux of Tennessee, who told the Democrats in 1960, ''I would just like to know if Mr. Chamberlain's venerable umbrella is being dusted off in anticipation of another Armageddon, where this nation, speaking too softly and too gently and too humbly, might crucify the hopes and aspirations of free men upon the cross of timidity''), let us push on to the nominating procedure. It is not thought proper merely to say that somebody has been nominated. He or she has to be placed in nomination. Thus for the Republicans in 1960 we had Governor Paul Fannin of the great state of Arizona rising on the platform for the purpose of placing in nomination the name of a great American as president of the United States of America. That is the full orchestration. Fannin placed in nomination rather than simply nominating, and he placed a name in nomination, which compounded the redundancy, something that is always admired at conventions.

Another approach to nominating is the alliterative. In 1960 Mark Hatfield, then governor of Oregon, nominated, or placed in nomination, Richard Nixon, describing him as one who had demonstrated courage in crisis from Caracas to the Kremlin. Hatfield produced five hard c sounds — courage in crisis from Caracas to the Kremlin — and plainly exhausted himself in the process, for the best he could do after that was to say that Nixon also had earned the affection and respect of millions from Ghana to Warsaw, which was not alliterative and did not rhyme either.

Hatfield remains, nonetheless, unchallenged. Seconding Hubert Humphrey's nomination in 1968, Governor Kenneth Curtis of Maine fell well short with character, courage, and compassion. He would have had to add his own name, Kenneth Curtis, to equal Hatfield's record.

Another approach is the immaterial. When the Democrats met in Los Angeles in 1960, one of the Missouri delegates introduced the great governor of the great state of Missouri, James G. Blair, Jr., who then proceeded to point out that there were five states between Missouri and the Atlantic Ocean, and five states between Missouri and the Pacific Ocean; two states between Missouri and Canada, and two states between Missouri and Mexico. That led him to conclude that Missouri was the heart of the Motherland of America, which made it logical that Governor Blair should nominate for president a man from the heart of America, who was Senator Stuart Symington of Missouri.

The more habitual approach to nominating and seconding is the declamatory:

"History will record the greatness of his administration. As it is inscribed upon the permanent page, so it is etched in the minds and hearts of a grateful people."

"But his warmth and compassion and sense of justice are implicit in the entire range of his record in public life."

"Mr. Chairman, I proudly rise tonight to confirm a commitment that was wrought in the crucible of another era."

"It is the worst of times that calls for the best in men."

"Destiny has again marked this man. A man to match our mountains and our plains. A man steeped in the glorious traditions of the past. A man with a vision of the unlimited possibilities of a new era."

This last was said at the Republican convention in 1968, which also produced a man for all seasons and two legends in their own time.

The clergymen who open and close the convention sessions get into the spirit and sound as though *they* are making nominating speeches:

"We are assembled in trying times that test the souls of men."

After the nominations come the demonstrations for the various candidates, which, to the regret of almost nobody except the musicians and others who were paid to take part in them, are not what they used to be. The only memorable thing that ever happened to me during a demonstration came in Los Angeles in 1960, when I ventured out during the demonstration for Kennedy. The first person I saw was the actress, which is stretching things a bit, Zsa Zsa Gabor. She had met the governor of a southwestern state, and she was telling him that she had a soft spot for that state because she had once been married there. That did not make the state exactly unique, but the governor seemed grateful.

It is the roll calls that bring forth the strongest expressions of measured ecstasy. It is permissible for the chairman of a delegation to say merely that his state casts so many votes for so-and-so, and occasionally that does happen. Some chairmen are content to say that their states proudly cast, or are proud to cast, so many votes for so and so. Beyond that point there is no holding back. States may cast their votes in the proud tradition of the independent man. They may couple their pride with another emotion, so that Michigan may be proud and honored, Minnesota may feel pride and satisfaction and New Jersey pride and enthusiasm, while the Virgin Islands may do its voting proudly and unanimously, this being made easier by its having only one delegate.

States like to point out their distinguishing qualities during the roll calls — Virginia, mother of presidents; Arizona, most promising state of the union; Florida, the original and unequaled sunshine state, which may draw boos from California, the other original and unequaled sunshine state; the beloved island state of Hawaii, where East meets West in the spirit of aloha; the beautiful-sky state of Colorado, not to be confused with Montana, the Big Sky country; North Dakota, the only state with an international peace garden, which is also North Dakota, the state that is cleaner and greener in the summer, and whiter and brighter in the winter; Vermont, the Green Mountain state; Washington, the only state in the union named after George Washington; the District of Columbia, where the White House is; Tennessee, the great Volunteer State and home of Andrew Jackson (for Democrats only); Wonderful Wyoming, which may also point with pride to its grant of legal equality to women ("The first state to recognize you lovely ladies''); Montana, "the first state to send a woman to Congress"; Delaware, "the first state to ratify the Constitution"; Nebraska, "the football capital of the world"; and Guam, "where America's day begins."

States may boast of their worth to the party that is holding the convention. I have heard Vermont say it had voted Republican for one hundred and four years; Illinois that a hundred years before, it was the state of Abraham Lincoln; North Dakota that it was traditionally Republican; Kansas that it was the most Republican state in the union; and Mississippi that it was the fastest growing Republican state in the country. On another roll call, Mississippi settled for being the home of two past Miss Americas, but that provoked a crushing reply from Utah, the home of Miss Universe. At the 1968 Democratic convention, Pennsylvania reached for immortality as the state where Senator Edmund Muskie's father worked in the coal mines.

Rivalry is everywhere and arises over

what may seem to the rest of us not fighting issues. One competition went this way:

Nevada — native state of Richard Nixon's wife.
Ohio — native state of Richard Nixon's father.
Oregon — neighbor of native state of Richard Nixon.

Another rivalry pitted Puerto Rico, "a bulwark against communism in the troubled waters of the Caribbean Sea," against the Virgin Islands, "your pearls in the Caribbean and America's tropical playground." Later, evidently out of sheer exuberance, the Virgin Islands threw in that it was "the southeasternmost real estate under the American flag" and the "home of the world-record blue marlin."

The 1972 Democratic convention in Miami Beach was organized under the McGovern-Fraser rules that brought women, blacks, Chicanos, Indians, the young, the old, and the poor as delegates in unprecendented numbers. A vice-chairperson presided much of the time and California had a co-chairperson; Spanish was spoken from the platform ("Yo exhorto a los delegados a derrotar este asalto a la justicia Americano"), and at one point it was announced, "The Chicano-Latino caucus is now being held in the Dolphin Room"; the delegates were asked to get with it; and under the heading of sexual orientation there was a debate on a gay rights plank, with one proponent claiming to represent "20,000,000 gay women and men who are looking for a political party that is responsive to their needs" and another beginning her speech: "I am Madeline Davis. I am an elected delegate from the Thirty-seventh Congressional District in Buffalo, New York. I am a woman. I am a lesbian."

In this atmosphere, rivalry took a different tack and, as the roll calls went along, was measured in disdain for nonunion lettuce:

"The Oregon delegation, which boycotted nonunion grapes in 1968, and which now supports the United Farm Workers' boycott of nonunion lettuce . . ."

"New York's delegation, which supports the boycott of nonunion lettuce . . ."

"New Jersey, another state which boycotts nonunion lettuce . . ."

"New York, the largest state that continues to boycott lettuce . . ."

"New Mexico, which has a lettuce boycott . . ."

"Idaho, where we, the Chicanos, also boycott nonunion lettuce . . ."

"Colorado, which fully supports the United Farm Workers' boycott of lettuce . . ."

"The District of Columbia, whose delegation here will eat no lettuce until the United Farm Workers tell us . . ."

"The Oregon delegation, which has demonstrated support for the lettuce boycott by not eating lettuce served on the United Airlines plane, at this convention, throughout our state, and at the hotel . . ."

"The Arizona delegation, which

supports the United Farm Workers . . ."

"California casts 131 votes yes, 114 votes no, 26 not voting. Oh, and we don't eat lettuce."

It is not unheard of for states, as they proudly cast their votes, to drum up a little business en route. Arkansas may recommend its razorback hogs, Idaho its potatoes, Kansas its wheat, Alabama its Birmingham 500 automobile race, Florida the Daytona 500, New Hampshire its granite, Delaware its Delaware-Marvelous chickens. And the competition for tourism can be fierce among South Dakota, home of Mount Rushmore; beautiful, wonderful, friendly West Virginia; North Carolina, the summer land where the sun doth shine; Minnesota, the land of ten thousand lakes; Colorful Colorado; Vermont, the eastern vacation capital; New Hampshire, the scenic land of America; Rhode Island, America's first vacation land; Michigan, the water, winter wonderland, and the arsenal of democracy to boot; Wisconsin, America's dairy land and the vacation land of the Midwest; New Mexico, the land of enchantment; and the great pine tree state, America's vacation state, the home of the Maine lobster and the Maine potato, a state eventually revealed to be Maine. Missouri once entered the lists as "the state with everything."

Gratifying as the opportunity to say such things may be to those who say them, the overwhelming majority of delegates never address the convention. They will, if there is nothing better to do, pay a certain amount of attention to the speeches, enough so that on certain key words — This great party, We will win in November, Franklin D. Roosevelt (for Democrats only) — they clap hands and cheer. Given clues of sufficient clarity, they also boo. When there is a pause, they may cheer mechanically, on the assumption that the speaker expects it and that is why he paused.

Many words go by without being noticed. Nuclear holocaust does not cause a ripple. In the Jeffersonian tradition — no reaction. We say to the Communists we accept your challenge to peaceful competition — silence. We cannot shirk this challenge and we will not shirk this challenge — not a stir. Sterile, unsound, and doomed to failure, a description of the opposing party's policies — silence. This is no ordinary convention; this will be no ordinary election; for these are no ordinary times — nothing. We are proud of our record, but we will not rest on it or be content with past performance — nothing again.

A recurrent theme at conventions is We can, we must, and we shall. When the Democrats met in 1972, Governor Reubin Askew of Florida made it, "I submit that we can, I submit that we must, and I submit that we shall." The official proceedings of the convention note that he was applauded for this, and I am in no position to dispute this, since I do not remember. However, it is a rare speech that stirs the delegates. Except when something big is going on, the convention floor is a combination social hall and lounge. The delegates meet their friends, read papers and magazines, write letters, have their pictures taken with well known politicians, and carry on conversations. One of the most popular spots for conversations is just below the speakers' platform. At times you wonder why they don't set up a table tennis tournament.

Those who are interested in convention language are better advised to stay at home and trust to radio and television than to try to hear it at the convention itself, as the following poignant passage shows:

"Delegate from the state of Nevada — 'Mr. Chairman, we had been prepared to place in nomination for Vice-President of these United States the name of Lieutenant Governor Rex Bell, Nevada's favorite son and Silver Statesman of the Silver State, but now that Richard Nixon has been officially chosen as our standard-bearer in 1960 we are abandoning this plan in deference to our favorite daughter and your favorite daughter, Pat Nixon, a native of America's last Free State. Therefore, Nevada passes.'

"The Secretary of the Convention — 'I wish more people could have heard that.

If the people would please be quiet, you could hear some of these beautiful words being spoken.' "

4

Not to Worry, Gold Stick, Old Chap

During breakfast one morning in a hotel in the English south coast resort of Bournemouth, these words came floating across the dining room: "I do hope Nanny is able to stop Giles fiddling with himself before he goes away to school."

It would be pleasant to report that the other guests rose as one, applauded, and shouted "Hear, hear," or that a kindly psychologist happened to be present and sent the woman a discreet note explaining that the latest studies suggested there was no cause for alarm: "Perfectly normal, madam. Healthy juvenile curiosity about the self. Only to be expected." In fact, nothing happened. Breakfast went on. The Bournemouth hotel where Giles's fiddling was made public knowledge clung to such gentility as it could, and in such places the propensity of the British upper classes, or would-be upper classes, to speak as though nobody else is present, at any rate nobody worthy of notice, is well known. It must have evolved in the days when prosperous Britons were constantly surrounded by servants and there would have been no conversation at all if nothing personal had been said until the servants had gone.

The practice does surprise the stranger, however, on first encounter. I had been in Britain only a few days when, in a hotel elevator, I heard one of two women tell the other about her recent marriage. Her husband, on seeing her two dozen pairs of shoes for the first time, had said, "But surely these are not all necessary," and she had triumphantly replied, "Of course they are not all necessary." Hotel elevators, since they are enclosed and are likely to contain strangers, offer ideal sites for such pronouncements. In that same elevator, a woman looked at me, looked at her husband, and said, "Timothy, here is a man who is taller than you are." Timothy appeared to take this intelligence in good part, though whether he later gave way to despair can only be surmised. As with the outcome of Giles's fiddling, we shall never know.

The confidence with which such people speak, the disdain for others, and, among women working for airlines, for example, the disembodied voice cultivated at British charm schools lead many Americans to stand in awe of the British use of English. There is no reason for Americans to feel inferior to the British when it comes to language. The British are as intent on ruining theirs as we are on ruining ours. Americans should also understand that most Britons who come to the United States, sounding polished, are from the upper and middle classes. Lower-class British accents, which are seldom heard here, are appalling.

An American inferiority complex is without justification, if only because

British English is fed by the stream of American English. The British leap at the trite and banal and make them their own with the same avidity as Americans. You cannot spend a day in Britain without hearing game plan, becoming operative, image, think tank, nitty-gritty, rapping, for real, and other afflictions that the United States has exported.

On August 17, 1973, Thorn Electrical Industries announced in London that it was dissolving a partnership with GTE International. Thorn said: "The original expectation of broad market penetration of the United Kingdom market has not been met in the time-frame contemplated, and the two companies have now decided that their objectives will be better served by separately owned activities."

That could not be more authentic, even to the slightly offline idea of serving an objective. At times, however, the Americanism undergoes a sea change. The British have taken over the personality weather forecaster, but he is an employe of the Meteorological Office, not of the television network. He is understandably cautious, but conversational, so that he may say, "I'm going to use a broad brush tonight and not be very exact," and he may note, "There's a bit of fog about," and instead of the old stand-bys, bright periods and sunny intervals, he may speak of gleams of sunshine or the odd chink of blue. But while he is sympathetic and homely, he does not smile, and when the weather belies his forecasts, he does not laughingly take personal responsibility for unexpected storms and icy patches on the roads or explain that his weekend, too, was ruined. This is just as well. Hearty humor about wintry showers, freezing fog, and gale-force winds would only make things worse.

Many Americanisms are distorted during export. A correspondent for British Independent Television News thought that the Conservative Party leader, Edward Heath, talking to people outside Boots the Chemist in Nottingham, was on a whistle-stop tour. "Let them," the head of the British policemen's union said during a recent wage dispute, "put their money where their sentiments lie."

The British can be as stubborn about pronunciation as they are in their belief that Chicago and other places away from the East Coast constitute the provinces. They rejoice to think that Layonard Bairnshtine is in London or Manchester as a guest conductor, possibly with Eezock Shtairn as violin soloist. They still think kindly of American commanders of NATO, but to them General Lauris Norstad was Norshtadt, and General Alfred Gruenther, who came from Platte Center, Nebraska, was given a Wagnerian pronunciation that might have put him on the German General Staff. The BBC may quote a comment from Washington by Markee Childs of the *St. Louis Post-Dispatch,* perhaps on the case of Spy'ro Agnew or that of John Air'lich'mann.

In 1972 the BBC, secure in its own view of American life, was convinced that the World Series was being played by the Pittsburgh Pirates and the Baltimore Creoles. Still, many Britons think it a mark of generosity to learn American names at all. My daughter was a student at Oxford at the time of the 1964 American presidential election. When word came in that President Johnson had won, one of her tutors said to her, "Better than thingummy, I suppose."

This last attitude intimidates some Americans, and their feeling of inferiority may be reinforced by the success of British plays in the United States. When American plays succeed in London, it is more likely to be put down to their "vigor" and "revelation of human emotion" than to their ideas or the high quality of their language, which are what British plays are usually credited with over here. Why this exaggerated respect for British plays persists, I — after six seasons of examining the relevant evidentiary material — cannot tell you.

Winston Churchill is credited with saying that the fact that the United States and Great Britain speak the same language is the most significant fact of the twentieth century. When I was reviewing plays, there were many nights when, for me, Churchill's significant fact had its drawbacks. Thus I saw *How the Other Half Loves,* which was about moronic married couples living in the suburbs and fighting, getting drunk, throwing food at each other, using electric toothbrushes that didn't work, having misunderstandings on the telephone, and putting antiperspirant in the soup. The child of the family played grocery with his father's shoes and left a tomato in one of them. Why it was thought necessary to supplement American mass production of comedies about moronic married couples in the suburbs I never did figure out.

One citation is hardly conclusive, but there was also *Not Now, Darling,* billed as a "romp," in which the audience could tell the leading actor was funny because he had a funny name, Arnold Crouch. Sample dialogue: "Mr. Crouch, where are you going?" "Out of my mind."

There was also *The Flip Side,* in which two married couples swap partners one night and nasal repartée all evening, and — I'll skip the names — there were comedies that relied on military officers going about without trousers, comedies of marital infidelity, comedies of mistaken identity, comedies of marital infidelity and mistaken identity combined, and more, many more.

Canada's English-speaking population one night opened a northern front by sending us a play called *A Minor Adjustment,* about a businessman who did not want his son to marry early and who, through his public relations man, hired a spirited girl artist to break up the affair. In the process the son became a hippie, and in the process we heard such jokes as "Try to pay a woman a compliment and she'll ask for a certified check" and "I know you're not kidding, boss, but I'd like to ask you a question: Are you kidding?"

Critics have no business feeling sorry for themselves, though it is an occupational hazard, but one reason I felt that I should not be so set upon by the British and the Canadians was that I was already receiving the attentions of American playwrights. Consider the plays that follow. They are not listed in any particular order, and, as you will see, there is no reason they should be.

Come Live with Me. About an American screen writer in London. Danish girl says, "I am Danish and I am finished." Drunken screen writer says, "God save the weasel. Pop goes the Queen."

Happily Never After. About two married couples. One husband throws up when he is troubled, the other complains that his wife is not reliable about taking birth control pills, while she explains that his ostentatious gargling with mouthwash is killing her love. Sample line: "Do you think when I'm up there sleeping, I'm sleeping?"

Love in E Flat. A young intern, jealous of his girl friend, bugs her apartment, while she deceives him into believing that she is pregnant and about to marry somebody else. Sample: "It is remarkable how inheriting a bank can make a man look like Richard Burton."

Lovely Ladies, Kind Gentlemen. Musical adaption of *The Teahouse of the August Moon.* The Americans bluff and innocent, and the natives, as it was compulsory to call them, quaint and innocent. The natives said "Okey-dokey," "Knock it off," and "Scram."

Another City, Another Land. About a hairdresser of integrity who conducts a hopeless fight against curls, waves, and wigs, and winds up on a street corner giving out religious tracts.

Lime Green and *Khaki Blue.* A double bill. In the first, a boy from Arkansas and a girl from New York come together, each intent on a first sexual experience. The boy is fixated on the color lime green. In the second, a woman of the evening remembers her innocence through an alcoholic haze and recalls a man whose eyes she thought were khaki blue.

The Mother Lover. A comedy about an aged woman and her son who hate each other. The son urges the mother to die, so that he will not have to support her, for then he and his wife, whom he also hates, could afford a live-in maid.

Something Different. A playwright re-creates in his house the conditions in which he wrote his only work — his mother's kitchen, complete with cockroaches and a large actress who impersonates his mother and comforts him by shoving his head into her bosom.

The Ninety Day Mistress. A sexually emancipated young woman picks up a young man and offers him ninety days of cohabitation. She is free with her favors because her father deserted her pregnant mother twenty-five years earlier. She and the young man fall in love. The father comes back.

The Song of the Grasshopper. A Spanish play, adapted, about a lovable ne'er-do-well in Madrid who lives in a house where rain comes through the roof and who smokes a pipe to show that he is happy.

A Time for the Gentle People. A former football star in Mississippi, now a drunken repairman in a tenement in Hell's Kitchen, sits fully clothed in a bathtub, quoting Shakespeare. His brother, the mayor of Biloxi, thinks his brother's name can help him become governor and has found him a job as a football coach. Should the repairman go back?

The Impossible Years. A psychiatrist is unable to control his own daughter. Psychiatrically oriented line: "He worships the ground your couch is on." Nonpsychiatrically oriented line: "Those cigarette butts will stay on the carpet until it dies of nicotine poisoning."

Great Scot! A musical about Robert Burns, who makes his poetic bent evident early by singing "As long as there's a star, the answer can't be far." A cow gives birth, offstage, sound only.

Anya. A musical based on the story of Anatasia. Dauntless but melancholy peasants, melancholy but dauntless aristocrats, stern but gracious royalty, devil-may-care cossacks.

Agatha Sue, I Love You. "A lot of people would like to change places with you." "Well, if you can arrange it, make it one of the Rockefellers."

The Happy Time. A musical with French Canadian characters who frequently advise each other that they are luckee and happee.

The Star Spangled Girl. A former

Olympic swimmer gets mixed up with the editors of a left-wing magazine who have published an article on twenty-seven ways to burn a wet draft card. The AP is confused with the A & P, and ball point pens are ruined in an automatic pencil sharpener.

For Love or Money. A musical comedy about a family in Italy trying to marry off a son to an American girl. "Now we're cooking with mozzarella." Lyrics: "My heart is full of sorrow, We're almost on the morrow," "If you cheat at love's game, You take the blame," "While I'm in my prime, Let me taste that heavenly wine."

The Rothschilds. "They are ruthless men who will stop at nothing."

Two by Two. About Noah's ark. When the flood comes, Noah sings "The God I Know Will See Us Through" in march tempo.

Soon. Rock opera. "I wanna know who puts the poison in the sea, I wanna know why the people still aren't free." Showed the influence of the environmental movement on the theater.

The Best Laid Plans. A playwright needs disturbed women as material to work into his plays. A girl pretends to a variety of delinquencies and captures his heart. "You are a narcissi." "What is a narcissi?" "A narcissi is a flower that doesn't like girls."

Ari. Adapted from the book *Exodus.* "We bagged that blockade runner." "Jolly good."

All the plays mentioned, British as well as American, were seen in New York, after I had ceased to work in Britain and after my attitude toward that country and its language was formed. Still, whatever I thought of the plays, I was glad to hear "Jolly good" in the last one. I had gone to London expecting to hear it shower down on all sides, but it was rarely used. I learned early that it was a mistake to look for such constants in the way the British use language. Instead, there were fads.

At this moment, for example, bloody-minded, once used only occasionally, is a fad. Bloody-minded is used principally in industrial disputes, but also to condemn the attitude of anyone who will not give way to your point of view. The high and mighty and the socially prominent use it to show that they are both democratic and with it. If they can work it in somehow, they will show that they are even more with it by referring to the place where they live as their pad.

Nonetheless, there are a few granitic eternals in the British language. One is the cough, one is the giving of leads, and one is the code. There are many coughs in Britain: the discreet clearing of the throat by the butler when he interrupts the master in some dubious activity or nodding over the family's deteriorating accounts; the cigarette smoker's rasp; the concertgoer's convulsion, which can drown out the entire series of trumpet calls in the *Leonore* Overture Number Three. I am thinking, however, of a businesslike bark, almost universal, and favored by a climate that makes practice possible all year round. Justice Potter Stewart of the United States Supreme Court said about pornography that he could not define it but he knew it when he saw it. The all-England hack is like that:

people know it when they hear it, and it is a sign to any Briton within hearing that a countryman is present. It is a morale-builder and a reassurance.

This all-England hack, I believe, holds the explanation of that curious institution, the English Sunday. It is not now as determinedly gloomy as it was in the days when the Church of England flourished and Sunday Observance was one of the consequences, but even now many a visitor, walking the deserted streets, has wondered what is going on behind the curtained windows. The answer is simple: the generations have gathered for a family cough.

The second constant is the conviction, held by all shades of political opinion, that the world is looking to Britain for "a lead." This persists today, though less aggressively, but when I lived in England, from 1949 to 1957, it shocked Americans, who believed that supplying leads was their province. One of the first leads I ever saw given was handed down by Princess Elizabeth before she became queen. She made — or read — a speech in which she argued that there was much to be said for an old-fashioned view of the family and for family life, and advised her listeners not to be afraid of being called prudes. A well-known Sunday paper at once rushed into the streets with a special article headed: Princess Elizabeth Gives Us a Lead.

One difficulty is that while leads are given freely, they are less often taken, which has a way of provoking disagreements. Sometime in the 1950s, when John Foster Dulles was secretary of state, the American and British governments were extremely angry with each other about something in the Middle East and exchanged insults and acrimony. A member of the Foreign Office was asked about the situation. He was a diplomat of the old school. "Merely the projection of a long-standing difference of emphasis," he said.

His blandness notwithstanding, the British were highly displeased that they had gone to the trouble of giving a lead that was not being followed. However, as their influence diminished they became

221

accustomed to doing this and soon drew satisfaction from having their leads ignored, because that showed how perverse and shortsighted other people were who didn't know a lead when they saw one. The British still give leads, but not in the manner of a great power. Their leads now are in such fields as showing self-discipline and setting disinterested examples. These have even less chance of being followed than the other kind.

I remember the Labor Defense Minister, Emanuel Shinwell, in the early 1950s doing something that displeased Winston Churchill, and Churchill snapping at him, "Oh, go and talk to the Italians. That is all you are good for." Now, their confidence sapped by economic troubles, the British warn each other that if things don't pick up they may well have a growth rate lower than Italy's. This is quite a comedown. They even warn each other that if they don't follow this or that policy, they will sink to the economic level of Portugal. This is a far cry from giving a lead.

It is also insulting to Portugal, which, at

least until the 1974 coup, appeared not to mind being held up as an object lesson in abjectness. The British, however, do not stop even at Portugal. They warn each other that if they are not careful they may well have inflation on the scale of a banana republic. This implies that the British still believe it is in the natural order of things for them to be superior to Portugal and banana republics, though how long that confidence will last nobody can say. Why it is nobler to export Scotch and gin (and be a gin monarchy) than it is to export coffee, tea, sugar, spices, and bananas the British appear not to have asked themselves.

As a matter of fact, the British once seemed to me to want to become a worm and chair monarchy. I covered an exposition of British goods in New York at which they were selling worms. The worms, of course, did come from what Shakespeare called "this blessed plot, this earth, this realm, this England." No other worms could make that claim. The exposition also contained a pub called The Red Lion. Here the visitor was able to sit

223

in a replica of a chair used by Mary, Queen of Scots. Why beer should taste better if the drinker is sitting in a replica of a chair used by a martyred queen was not clear. The British may have thought it would appeal to the much-publicized sentimentality of Americans.

One of the many fields in which the British thought they were giving the world a lead was in density of bonnie babies in proportion to the population. This homely phrase was refurbished at each election, general and by-, as we do with sovereign state and these United States. The party in power claimed that the babies of the country had never been so bonnie, thanks to the enlightened policies of the party in power, while the opposition party claimed that the babies' bonnieness, though undeniable, arose from *its* earlier period in office when reforms leading directly to bonnieness were instituted, and furthermore that they would be bonnier still if the opposition got back in. This rivalry did not end until the British became more interested in the bonnieness of houses, cars, and holidays abroad.

The third common denominator was the use of code. We were in a London theater watching a Sean O'Casey play in which he made fun of British landowners in Ireland when two Irishmen whom I took to be construction workers — navvies is the British word — and who had obviously stopped off en route to fortify themselves, commenced contributing their own anti-British lines to the performance. Soon the theater manager and the commissionaire came down the aisle. (Army sergeants from the First World War formed a corps of commissionaires to be employed as doormen-guards-receptionists.)

"All right, lads. Come along now," said the commissionaire.

The Irishmen understood the code — leave quietly or the police will be along and there will be trouble none of us want but which you in particular don't want. They rose and left.

What appears to be gentle treatment often isn't, if you know the code. You will see members of Parliament described as respected, highly respected, well loved, popular, colorful and flamboyant. The

225

first four categories are self-explanatory, although well loved usually means, in truth, that the M.P. is old and has been around for a long time and is no longer effective. Colorful means that the M.P. works too hard at attracting attention, and flamboyant means that everybody would be happier if he went away. If a newspaper reports that a politician was tired while making a speech or appearing on television, the meaning is that the politician had been drinking. If the politician was very tired, he should not have been out in public at all.

This restraint about politicians, with which libel laws may have much to do, often is not matched among the politicians themselves. In the House of Commons, known in some journalistic circles as the Mother of Parliaments and when there is any disorder as the normally staid Mother of Parliaments, there are well-established measures of the response of members to a speech or statement — sympathetic noises in all parts of the House, cries of "Hear, hear," cheers, loud cheers, prolonged cheers, and waving of papers. There may also be hostile noises, groans, and shouts of "Resign." After this, individual initiative takes over with "Sit down," "Belt up," "Shut up," "Get stuffed," "Knock off," "Put a sock in it," "Disgraceful," "He's drunk" and "Cock-a-doodle-doo."

When I arrived in London in 1949 I was astonished by the hooting to which the Laborites in the House of Commons subjected Conservatives. Labor, of course, was riding high in those days, and at the beginning of that Parliament one of its members, Hartley Shawcross, had made a well-publicized remark to the Conservatives: "We are the masters now." Shawcross, a lawyer and one of the prosecutors at the Nuremberg War Crimes Tribunal, later became Lord Shawcross and prominent in the financial district, the City of London. He may have felt the same way there.

Conservatives are more vulnerable to hooting and to the salutations listed above because so many of them affect an upperclass stammer. Actually, it is not so much a stammer as it is the repetition of certain words — and and but, principally — and the frequent insertion of "Errr," said in a rather distant way. Whatever the reason for it — to give the impression that the precise word is being searched for, to show that haste is unseemly, to build up drama by making the audience wait — it does give those listening a chance to make their own comments.

The House of Commons prides itself on the level of its debates, and it can be cruel. Near the end of his career, the Labor politician Herbert Morrison made a speech on economic policy in which he said, "If it were just a little matter that didn't matter, it would be another matter." Groans went up all over the House, first because of the banality of the statement, second because Morrison was still hoping to become leader of the Labor party. He had only an outside chance and the speech killed it.

As a politically suicidal comment, it ranked with Prime Minister Harold Macmillan's comment on the Profumo scandal of 1962 - 63. "All got up by the press," said Macmillan, thereby propelling himself into the twilight of his career. Another consequential remark was Winston Churchill's in the 1945 election campaign that if the Socialist ministers in his wartime coalition cabinet came to power, Britain would have a Gestapo. Some years later there was the Laborite Aneurin Bevan's "The organized workers of this country are our friends. As for the rest, they are lower than vermin." You don't say that kind of thing in a two-party system and have much chance of becoming prime minister.

Stuck with their upper-class stammer, the Conservatives often dream of finding working-class candidates to run under their banner (though not for safe seats). At the first Conservative party conference I went to, in 1950, a man named Anthony Bulbrooks was introduced. He mounted the platform, thrust out his hands, palms toward the audience, and announced, "I work with these." The cheers were stupendous, and the trapper who found Bulbrooks and brought him in was probably paid a bounty.

There was nothing like it for years afterward until one of the more erratic spirits among the Tories, Quintin Hogg, came up on the platform with an enormous bell, which he rang while he shouted a message to Labor: "Ask not for whom the bell tolls. It tolls for thee."

You will hear Cockney and Midlands ("Ee, lad") and other accents at Labor party conferences, but not all the Laborites are horny-handed sons of toil, and expressions of pride in "our working-class movement" delivered in Oxford English by people born to privilege are a Bulbrookian equivalent. There are, also, few things as incongruous as the party leaders standing on the platform at the end of the conference, linking arms and singing "The Red Flag." After that, their revolutionary duty done, they — lawyers, academicians, managers, professional politicians, journalists, trade-union officials, businessmen — go home.

To me the most characteristic moment at Labor party conferences was the moment of the emergence of the composite resolution, which is pronounced with a long i and the accent on the last syllable. It was then said, when a number of resolutions had been brought together into one, that they had been composited. For party functionaires able to say this, it was the high point of the year.

Another part of the British code is the hyphenated name. Among no other people is the hyphen so imaginatively used. British hyphenation preserves the bride's name, though not as an early example of equality for women but rather as a signal that two dynasties had been joined. It results for the most part in prosaic names like Hornsby-Smith and Gordon-Walker, but rises to a higher level of inspiration with Finch-Knightley and Fox-Strangways and Lowry-Corry, and occasionally produces a national treasure like Buller-Fullerton-Elphinstone and Money-Coutts.

The British peerage pours new names into use because it needs regular infusions of recruits if it is to be kept going. Somebody who has been Reginald Edward Manningham-Buller all his life, for example, may disappear and reemerge, at the age of fifty-nine, as Lord Dilhorne. This keeps everybody alert.

Since 1964 no hereditary peerages have been created, only life peerages, which become extinct when the new peer or peeress does; the title cannot be handed on. Among the life peers there is a tendency to keep their own names and so to become Lady Burton or Lord Sorenson, or whatever it may be. Sometimes they also keep their first names and insert a hyphen where none has been before. Thus Lord George-Brown made up for the loss of Manningham-Buller's hyphen, above. When the government of Prime Minister Heath created a new batch of life peers after dissolving Parliament and calling an election in early 1974, one of those ennobled was the politician Duncan Sandys. He became a baron and in this new eminence felt the need of a hyphen. He therefore changed his name by deed poll to Duncan Duncan-Sandys. (The y is silent and the pronunciation is Sands, which adds to the general good cheer.)

I think that if I were British I would try to enter into the spirit of the thing by hyphenating my name by deed poll and making it, perhaps, Edwin Deed-Poll, or possibly Edwin Hyphen-Newman. I was dismayed to meet in Ghana the wife of a British official who was entitled to use four names and three hyphens but used only two and one respectively. This undermines the system.

By contrast, there lived in England Admiral the Honourable Sir Reginald Aylmer Ranfurly Plunkett-Ernle-Erle-Drax, who fought at Heligoland, Jutland, and Dogger Bank in the First World War, and was a convoy commodore in the Second. I deeply regretted that I was never able to include his name in a broadcast, or those of members of the Montagu-Stuart-Wortley-Mackenzie and Hovell-Thurlow-Cumming-Bruce families. One hyphen down, Lady Jane Vane-Tempest-Stewart made some headlines as a debutante. I never got her name on the air either.

The Admiral and the Lady had an embarrassment of hyphens, but noteworthy names can be made with a single hyphen, as Sir Humphrey

Dodington Benedict Sherston Sherston-Baker showed. For the British, the hyphen serves somewhat the same purpose as the accent. It is a bird call by which the species is identified. In British general elections, only the names of the candidates for Parliament are given, not their party affiliations. At the election of February, 1974, the son of a duke said that by the time he got inside the voting booth he often forgot which candidate was the Conservative. "In that case," he said, "I look for the name with a hyphen." If there was no hyphenated name, he said, "I look for a name such as Knox or Jones and vote against it."

There was a time when sons of dukes were expected to forget which candidate was the Conservative, and to forget everything else of consequence. Then, as they grew older and became dukes themselves, they were expected to potter about. Pottering about was considered a suitable occupation for someone in their position whose money came from land rather than commerce and who had the requisite breeding. Pottering ceased to be valued so highly when a more aggressive consumer society, imitating the American, took over. There used to be, for example, the tradition of genteel advertising, embodied by the notice that said, "If you know of a better toothpaste than Gordon-Moore's Satin Dental Cream, we should be glad to hear about it." I assume that people with hyphenated names would still lean to Gordon-Moore's, but advertising of such disinterested confidence is no more.

The British have a way of referring to certain well-known Americans, past and present, as Foster Dulles, Cabot Lodge, and Luther King, implying that a hyphen should be present. The hyphenated name has never caught on in the United States, but we do come close to it with a legacy of our own. This is the richness afforded society by the names of university and college presidents.

Take two well-known examples, one from the past — Nicholas Murray Butler, president of Columbia, 1902 - 45 — and one from the present, Kingman Brewster, president of Yale since 1964. Both names could be hyphenated without difficulty: "Sir Roger Nicholas-Murray-Butler said today that he was leaving the family banking firm to found . . ." and "Anthony Kingman-Brewster, son of the former British Ambassador to Iraq, is joining the Welsh commercial television company as an assistant producer."

But both names go well beyond hyphenability. Each is interchangeable within itself. Kingman Brewster. Brewster Kingman. Nicholas Murray Butler. Nicholas Butler Murray. Murray Nicholas Butler. Murray Butler Nicholas. Butler Murray Nicholas. Butler Nicholas Murray.

They are also interchangeable with each other. Nicholas Kingman Brewster. Brewster Nicholas Kingman. And so on and so on.

If you examine the names of American university and college presidents, past and present, you find this circular quality to a remarkable degree. In the Kingman Brewster style, there were, for example, Glenn Frank (University of Wisconsin, 1925 - 37) and Grayson Kirk (Columbia,

1953 - 68), though it should be noted that the field is so rich that while Kingman Brewster achieves interchangeability in four syllables, Grayson Kirk does it in three and Glenn Frank did it in two.

The Nicholas Murray Butler style of three interchangeable names represents the peak and occurs less commonly. James Russell Lowell (Harvard, 1909 - 33) was an early example, and among current presidents there are Lloyd Drexell Vincent of Angelo State University, Texas, whose name seems to me to mark him out for certain academic advancement, and Forrest David Mathews of the University of Alabama, and Bernard Tagg Lomas of Abion, in Michigan.

There is a third style in which an initial occurring either at the beginning of the name or in the middle comes into play. Thus R. Dudley Boyce of Golden West College, California, and Atlee C. Kepler of Hagerstown Junior College, Maryland, and Porter L. Fortune, chancellor of the University of Mississippi.

When I became aware of the unusual properties of university presidents' names, which I did at an early age, I noticed that some, even when they fell short of interchangeability, still had a striking quality. My favorite for sheer symmetry was Robert Maynard Hutchins (University of Chicago, 1929 - 45). For pyramidal symmetry it was Guy Stanton Ford (University of Minnesota, 1938 - 41). For rhythm and euphony, it was Dixon Ryan Fox (Union College, Schenectady, New York, 1934 - 45). One of Fox's predecessors, serving from 1802 to 1866, was Elithalet Nott, a name well worth reviving.

Still, as noted, the peak is represented by the interchangeable triple name, and to reach this peak there are five requirements. The first is being male; the second is having an Anglo-Saxon surname; the third is having an Anglo-Saxon family name, usually the mother's, as a middle name; the fourth, displaying it; and the fifth, living among people who do the same or at least do not consider doing so a laughable affectation. These requirements met, a university presidency should not be far off.

I now append a short list of American university and college presidents with interchangeable names, double, triple, and double with initial, to show how high the incidence of interchangeability is, and how widely scattered. The list is drawn, alphabetically by state, from the Yearbook of Higher Education for 1973. Note that I have not taken the easy way; there is nobody on the list with James or Charles as first or last name; college presidents named (at any point) Thomas, Stanley, Howard, Leonard, Benjamin, Frank, Paul, Lawrence, Francis, Wallace, Albert, Ernest, Willard, Frederick, Douglas, Martin, Harvey, Wesley, Herman, Henry, Gordon, Glenn, Seymour, Lewis, Russell, Oliver, Willis, Curtis — and such college presidents are legion, or Legion L. Legion — have likewise been eliminated. Note also that the names are interchangeable up, down, diagonally, taking every other name, every third, fourth, fifth, and so on, at random, and — for parlor game purposes

239

— any other way you can think of. In mixed clusters of three, especially when read or sung aloud, they are often enchanting.

Levi Watkins	Alabama State University Montgomery, Alabama
Woodfin P. Patterson	Jefferson Davis State Jr. College Brewton, Alabama
Imon E. Bruce	Southern State College Magnolia, Arkansas
Cornelius P. Haggard	Azusa Pacific College Azusa, California
Cordas C. Burnett	Bethany Bible College Santa Cruz, California
Higgins D. Bailey	California College of Podiatric Medicine San Francisco, California
Brage Golding	California State University San Diego, California
Gibb R. Madsen	Hartnell College Salinas, California

Terrel Spencer   Imperial Valley College
                              Imperial, California

Wiley D. Garner   Long Beach City College
                              Long Beach, California

Leadie M. Clark   Los Angeles Southwest
                                 College
                              Los Angeles, California

Burton W. Wadsworth   Victor Valley College
                              Victorville, California

Rexer Berndt   Fort Lewis College
                              Durango, Colorado

Dumont Kenny   Temple Buell College
                              Denver, Colorado

Thurston E. Manning   University of Bridgeport
                              Bridgeport, Connecticut

Cleveland L. Dennard   Washington Technical
                                 Institute
                              Washington, D. C.

T. Felton Harrison   Pensacola Jr. College
                              Pensacola, Florida

Culbreth Y. Melton   Emmanuel College
                              Franklin Springs, Georgia

J. Whitney Bunting   Georgia College
Milledgeville, Georgia

Pope A. Duncan   Georgia Southern College
Statesboro, Georgia

Prince Jackson, Jr.   Savannah State College
Savannah, Georgia

Forest D. Etheredge   Waubonsee Community
College
Sugar Grove, Illinois

Hudson T. Armerding   Wheaton College
Wheaton, Illinois

Beauford A. Norris   Christian Theological
Seminary
Indianapolis, Indiana

Landrum R. Bolling   Earlham College
Richmond, Indiana

Byrum E. Carter   Indiana University at
Bloomington
Bloomington, Indiana

Glennon P. Warford   Ellsworth Community
College
Iowa Falls, Iowa

Merne A. Harris   Vennard College
University Park, Iowa

Arley A. Bryant   Cloud County Community
         Jr. College
        Concordia, Kansas

Duke K. McCall   Southern Baptist Theological
         Seminary
        Louisville, Kentucky

Mahlon A. Miller   Union College
        Barbourville, Kentucky

Dero G. Downing   Western Kentucky
         University
        Bowling Green, Kentucky

Broadus N. Butler   Dillard University
        New Orleans, Louisiana

W. Ardell Haines   Allegany Community College
        Cumberland, Maryland

D. Deane Wyatt   Baltimore College of
         Commerce
        Baltimore, Maryland

Atlee C. Kepler   Hagerstown Jr. College
        Hagerstown, Maryland

J. Renwick Jackson   St. Marys College of Maryland
        St. Marys, Maryland

Randle Elliott   Bay Path Jr. College
        Longmeadow, Massachusetts

Wheeler G. Merriam	Franklin Pierce College Rindge, New Hampshire
Placidus H. Riley	St. Anselm's College Manchester, New Hampshire
Ferrel Heady	University of New Mexico Albuquerque, New Mexico
Prezell R. Robinson	St. Augustine's College Raleigh, North Carolina
Ferebee Taylor	University of North Carolina at Chapel Hill Chapel Hill, North Carolina
Laud O. Vaught	Northwest Bible College Minot, North Dakota
Garland A. Godfrey	Central State College Edmond, Oklahoma
Dolphus Whitten, Jr.	Oklahoma City University Oklahoma City, Oklahoma
Harris L. Wofford, Jr.	Bryn Mawr College Bryn Mawr, Pennsylvania
Lane D. Kilburn	King's College Wilkes-Barre, Pennsylvania
Mayo Bryce	Moore College of Art Philadelphia, Pennsylvania

Bertrand W. Hayward   Pennsylvania College of
                        Textiles and Science
                        Philadelphia, Pennsylvania

Hilton M. Briggs   South Dakota State University
                        Brookings, South Dakota

Powell A. Fraser   King College
                        Bristol, Tennessee

Odell Horton   Le Moyne-Owen College
                        Memphis, Tennessee

Spurgeon B. Eure   Southern College of Optometry
                        Memphis, Tennessee

Lloyd Drexell Vincent   Angelo State University
                        San Angelo, Texas

Fount W. Mattox   Lubbock Christian College
                        Lubbock, Texas

Granville M. Sawyer   Texas Southern University
                        Houston, Texas

Lyman B. Brooks   Norfolk State College
                        Norfolk, Virginia

Lambuth M. Clarke   Virginia Wesleyan College
                        Norfolk, Virginia

J. Wade Gilley   Wytheville Community College
                        Wytheville, Virgina

Thornton M. Ford	Tacoma Community College Tacoma, Washington
D. Banks Wilburn	Glenville State College Glenville, West Virginia
Irvin G. Wyllie	University of Wisconsin - Parkside Kenosha, Wisconsin
Tilghman Aley	Casper Community College Casper, Wyoming

It happens rarely, but sometimes both the university and its president have interchangeable names. Note in the preceding list Dumont Kenny of Temple Buell College in Denver, and Wheeler G. Merriam of Franklin Pierce College in Rindge, New Hampashire. J. Osborne Fuller was president of Fairleigh Dickinson University in Rutherford, New Jersey, for some years until December, 1973. Fairleigh Dickinson could just as easily have been president of J. Osborne Fuller University or Dickinson Fuller of Fairleigh J. Osborne. The name of the town, Rutherford, might also be brought in, but that way lies madness.

There is another unquenchable and growing source of interchangeable and impressive names — foundations, another American phenomenon that, like universities, produces a sort of American peerage. Here we find, for example, W. McNeill Lowry, formerly vice-president for policy and planning of the Ford Foundation, now its vice-president for humanities and the arts. It is not necessary, however, to go below the topmost level of administrators. Far from it:

F. Paschal Gallot of the Miranda Lux Foundation, San Francisco; Tilden Cummings, Continental Bank Charitable Foundation, Chicago; Thorwald J. Fraser, Anderson Foundation, Boise, Idaho; Tecla M. Virtue, Phillips Foundation, Los Angeles; Royce H. Heath, Allen-Heath Foundation, Chicago; Emory K. Crenshaw, Frances Wood Wilson Foundation, Decatur, Georgia; Cason J. Callaway, Jr., Pine Mountain Benevolent Foundation, Columbus, Georgia; Alden H. Sulger, Stone Trust

Foundation, New Haven, Connecticut; Lawton M. Calhoun, Savannah Foundation, Savannah, Georgia; Brannon B. Lesesne, Patterson-Barclay Memorial Foundation, Atlanta; and since it must be obvious that this can go on indefinitely, the following, hardly more than a smattering, given without affiliation:

Leighton A. Wilkie, Brice E. Hayes, Chapman S. Root, Sacket R. Duryee, W. Craig Keith, Danforth Helley, Delmar S. Harder, Campbell A. Harlan, Firman H. Hass, Miner S. Keeler II, Cleveland Thurber, Burrows Morley, J. Woodward Roe, Shaw Walker, Macauley Whiting, Hobson C. McGehee, Shields Warren, Girard B. Henderson, J. Seward Johnson, Moore Gates, Jr., W. Parsons Todd, S. Whitney Landon, G. Sealey Newell, Oakleigh L. Thorne, Campbell Rutledge, Hart Taylor, Schuyler M. Meyer, Jr., P. Mathis Pfohl, Malin Sorsbie, Stark S. Dillard and — to close — J. Clib Barton of the Doss T. Sutton Charitable Foundation, Fort Smith, Arkansas, and E. Blois du Bois of the du Bois Foundation, Scottsdale, Arizona.

Like E. Blois du Bois, though unlike J. Clib Barton, many foundation heads are heads of foundations that have the same name they do, suggesting that a name itself may have a powerful influence, that if you have an interchangeable name, the demands of good citizenship impel you toward foundation founding, if no university presidency is available, as a British name of weight propels one toward the House of Lords. However, since anyone whose name qualifies him to be a university president is simultaneously qualified to be a foundation head, inevitably there is traffic, and even competition, between the two worlds. Note in the list of university presidents the entry Landrum R. Bolling, Earlham College, Richmond, Indiana. After the list was compiled Bolling was named executive vice-president of the Lilly Endowment. Bolling was succeeded at Earlham by Franklin W. Wallin, who had been president of the Institute for World Order, Inc., a position he occupied while on leave from Colgate University, where he was dean and provost and, given his name, inexorably moving higher.

The best-known foundation head is, of course, McGeorge Bundy, of the Ford. In the days when Bundy was in the government, I used to have a fantasy about the instructions President Johnson gave him before sending him off on one of his numerous visits to Vietnam.

"Listen, McGeorge," Mr. Johnson would say, "I don't want you wasting time out there. I don't want you talking to just any McTom, McDick or McHarry."

It was thanks to a 1953 movie called *The Treasure of Kalifa* that I became aware of another style in American names, less orotund but no less evocative, and identifying its owners as surely as a hyphen does. It has not entirely survived the changes in movie-making of the last couple of decades, but it did lie in the mainstream of American film-making in its time. That was when the male stars had one-syllable first names. Not ordinary, unimaginative names, but names that served a purpose, that punched, that revealed.

The stars of *The Treasure of Kalifa* were Rod Cameron and Tab Hunter. To pronounce those names was to know what manner of men they were. They were laconic, tough, informal, no-nonsense Americans. Their names also disclosed the nature of the film. It was an action picture, perhaps even an all-action picture, set in the great outdoors. The leading characters, busily engaged in all-action, barely had time to grunt. These were ideal parts for Rod and Tab.

See the utility of this fashion: Take the film *Back to God's Country*. This was another action or all-action picture, set in the frozen North, and it also had two laconic, tough, informal, no-nonsense Americans, Rock Hudson and Steve Cochran. Rock, however, was plainly the hero, because his name preceded Steve's in the billing. Rock, in fact, was "in" the picture, while Steve only "co-starred" with Marcia Henderson.

This, I agree, is easy. A man who was "in" a picture was more likely to be the hero than a man who was merely co-starring with Marcia Henderson. Let us

251

suppose, therefore, that we did not know that the Rock came before the Steve. It would still have been possible to know at once that Rock was the hero: his name had only four letters while Steve's had five. Steve may have been laconic, tough, informal and no-nonsense, but he was not as laconic, tough, informal and no-nonsense as Rock. All of that the names made clear.

So far so good. But go back to *The Treasure of Kalifa*. Rod and Tab are both three-letter names, and their owners were billed together, on the same line. Who was the hero there? The answer had to be that both were heroes. They were more: they were tried and trusty friends. It is true that in the film itself their names were different, but it is pleasant to think of a scene in which they stand silently, one at each side of a corner of a house, gun drawn, unable to see the other side but knowing somebody is there.

This is the suspenseful dialogue:

ROD: Tab?
TAB: Rod?
ROD: Right, Tab, it's Rod.
TAB: Right, Rod, it's Tab.

Both men then emerge, holster their guns, and call each other "you old galoot."

There was, of course, a limit to the number of films in which the leading men could be friends, and for the most part the producers juggled plots and casts so that they did not have a man playing the villain who had the same number of letters in his name as the man playing the hero. But allowing for the worst, suppose that a producer had a four-letter villain already cast when he found no two- or three-letter hero available. Even in this extremity, the producer had a way out. His salvation was to use a hero whose four-letter name was less orthodox and more manly than the four-letter name of the villain. Thus in *The Great Sioux Uprising* Jeff Chandler triumphed over Lyle Bettger. But Jeff would hardly have had a chance against somebody named, let us say, Hook.

There is an additional point — that some names were works of genius. By way of illustration, a Biff could easily have given away two letters to, say, an Os and still come out on top. Nobody name of Biff's gonna get beat by nobody name of Os, leastwise not if they fight fair. Feller name of Lash LaRue, star of *Son of a Badman* (and not to be confused with Whip Wilson, star of *Crashin' Through*), might do it, specially with the help of his sidekick Fuzzy St. John and extra specially if Fuzzy's name gits shortened to Fuzz. Otherwise, cain't do hit nohow.

The ideal one-syllable name for an all-action film hero would have been Id, particularly when westerns began to be made with psychological overtones. We might have had Id Libido, playing a character whose life is warped because his Italian descent makes him the butt of jokes by crudely chauvinistic cowboys, shooting it out with String Greenberg as the first Jewish cowboy west of St. Louis and trying to show how tough he is. Both die in the shoot-out, which makes the point that we should all be brothers, while Dream O'Day, playing an heiress who wants to be useful and who runs a pioneering psychological counseling service in the Oklahoma Territory, mourns them both and sobs that she has failed. She is consoled by a Chinese laundryman who laughs at everything because that is expected of him but deep down understands all, including acupuncture. With the help of a gently humorous Catholic priest, Father Figure (played by the famous Irish actor, Spalpeen Gossoon), he makes her believe that continuing her psychological counseling service will be worthwhile. The curtain falls before she can become Oklahoma's first woman senator or fit in another appointment.

On the whole, it will be seen that when it comes to names, we can match the British at their own game, even without hyphens. What they do have that we do not is heraldry, the science of armorial bearings. Britain remains one of the few places left outside of crossword puzzles where queries of a heraldic nature arise in life's normal course. They are referred to the College of Arms, where the functionaries answer them with a straight face. (It is said that an American correspondent once called the College of Arms and identified himself as representing the *New York Heraldic Tribune,* but if so, this was plainly the work of a cad and it is no wonder the paper died.)

At the College of Arms, which is to say King's College of Heralds and Poursuivants of Arms in Ordinary, you can see and talk to the Richmond Herald — a man, not a publication, and to be addressed, once you get to know him, as Richmond — and the Garter King of Arms. (Somewhere here there lurks a joke about "My son the herald," but let it go.) Not, mind you, that Richmond Herald and Garter King of Arms are outstanding as titles go. On the whole, the best titles for all purposes are Gentleman Usher of the Black Rod and Gold Stick-in-Waiting, who are in the Queen's household.

They are known, less formally, as Black

Rod and Gold Stick, and I can almost hear a conversation between them as they stand, concealed from each other, while on a security round in a dark and musty corridor of Buckingham Palace:

BLACK ROD: Gold Stick?
GOLD STICK: Black Rod?
BLACK ROD: Not to worry, Gold
    Stick. It's Black Rod.
GOLD STICK: Not to worry, Black
    Rod. It's Gold Stick.

Both men then emerge, lowering their Black Rod and Gold Stick respectively, call each other "old chap," wish each other "cheerie-bye," and depart.

I suppose I have a soft spot for Britain. It was there, through appearances on the BBC and the commercial network, that I achieved my first recognition. I was standing outside the NBC offices in London one day when a car went by, stopped, and reversed. The driver rolled down the window, put his head out, and said he knew me, that he recognized me as a television face. After some effort, he recalled my name. Then he reached for his wallet and gave me his business card.

"We do very good interior decorating," he said. "We would like to have your business. Drop in anytime."

Once you have grown accustomed to this sort of adulation, it is not easy to do without.

That ends this small and random sample of experiences with British English and some of its American counterparts. If you know of a better small and random sample, I should be glad to hear about it.

5

The Capacity
to Generate
Language
Viability
Destruction

The business instinct is by no means to be sneered at. I have had only one moneymaking idea in my life. It came to me like a flash (though not from Mr. Tash, the manager of a jewelry store in Washington, D. C., after the Second World War, and the inspiration of a radio commercial which began, ''Now here's a flash from Mr. Tash — If you'll take a chance on romance, then I'll take a chance on you,'' meaning that he sold engagement and wedding rings on credit).

It came to me like a flash one day when I was thinking about the growth of the population and the domination of American life by the automobile.

I fell to wondering, as any red-blooded American would, how some money might be made from that combination of factors, and I conceived the idea that because walking as a pleasure was becoming a lost art, a great deal of money might be made by setting up a pedestrians' sanctuary, a place where people could walk. I saw in my mind's eye the name WALKORAMA, or STROLLATERIA, or something of the sort, and a place that would require little in the way of outlay or upkeep — just some space, grass, trees, and quiet. Obviously it would need a parking lot so that people could drive to it and park their cars before entering the walkorama to walk, and I intended to hold on to the parking concession for myself.

Nothing came of it. It was a typically footless newsman's dream, like the little weekly with which to get back to real people, dispense serene wisdom, and go broke, in Vermont.

I do not, therefore, sneer at the men and women of business. If they were not buying time on NBC, the world might or might not be a poorer place, but I would unquestionably be a poorer inhabitant of it.

However, the contributions of business to the health of the language have not been outstanding. Spelling has been assaulted by Duz, and E-Z Off, and Fantastik, and Kool and Arrid and Kleen, and the tiny containers of milk and cream catchily called the Pour Shun, and by products that make you briter, so that you will not be left hi and dri at a parti, but made welkom.

This book was originally typed on paper drawn from a "slide-out pak."

"You're saked," the angry Amtrak chief said. "I caught on to you in the nik of time. I don't know what it was, but something cliked. If it hadn't, an entire trainload of knikknaks would have been lost. You make me sik," he went on. "There has been no lak of understanding of you here. You've carried on like a high muky-muk, with assistants at your bek and call, but you're driving us to rak and ruin. You'd have us in hok up to our neks. You were hoping that I'd blow my stak and crak under the strain, but I won't. Pik up your money, pak your things, and go. I want you cheked out in an hour, by four. You thought that you could duk responsibility, that you were dealing with a bunch of hiks, and that we were stuk with you. You were playing with a staked dek. Well, in sixty minutes, I want you out of here, lok, stok and barrel."

"Sok it to him, boss," a Uriah-Heep-like character among the employes murmured. "He has no kik coming. He just couldn't hak it." He gave a quaklike laugh and fed himself from a tube of Squeez-a-snak.

Dik Windingstad (for it was indeed he) hardly knew how to respond, so shoked was he, so taken abak by the Amtrak chief's attak, so roked bak on his heels. He felt like a hokey goalie hit in the face by a puk off the stik of Bobby Hull, and the tik-tik-tok of the stately clok as it stood against the wall sounded in his ears like the sharp reports of ak-ak guns. His heartbeat quikened. Then he thought sardonically to himself, "The buk stops here," and his mood changed. "We've had some yaks," he thought. "I must have upset the peking order."

He glanced down at his finely tailored slaks, never again to be worn in these precincts. "I'll go," he said finally. "But not with my tail tuked between my legs, as you'd like. Hek, no. Lok me out, if you want to. Mok me. Someday you'll take a different tak. Someday I'll get in the last lik. All I can say now is good-by and — for some of you, anyway — good luk. Please forward my mail to Hamtramk."

Dik spun on his heel and made traks. Amtraks.

In many such monstrosities, the companies involved know what they are doing. In others they often do not, especially when it is a matter of grammar. New York remains the business capital of the United States, and on a typical day there you may pick up the *New York Times,* or that paragon of eastern sophistication, the *New Yorker*

263

magazine, and find a well-known Fifth Avenue jeweler telling the world that "The amount of prizes Gübelin has won are too numerous to be pure chance." I happen to know that this was a straw man Gübelin was knocking down because nobody had said it were pure chance. The sentiment in the circles I travel in was that the amount of prizes were fully deserved.

In the same advertisement Gübelin also gives us the following: "Sculpture II, an 18-carat white-gold ring with 24 diamond baguettes and two smoky quartzes, fancy cut, is a unique work of art to be worn on one finger, and without doubt rightly among the Gübelin creations that have taken the Diamonds-International Award." Turning the word rightly into a verb is no small achievement, but it should have been rightlies, so that the advertisement would read, ". . . and without doubt rightlies among the Gübelin creations that have taken the Diamonds-International Award."

Another possible verb is gübelin. "I have gübelined," he said, hanging his head, "and I no longer rightly among you, winners all of the Diamonds-International Award." He turned and walked falteringly toward the door.

"For a moment it seemed that the high priest, or Tiffany, was about to forgive him, but it was not to be. 'Go,' the Tiffany said, pointing to the outer darkness, 'go and gübelin no more.' "

The edition of the *Times* graced by Gübelin also had an advertisement from Wallach's, a men's clothing store. It was headed, "Portentious prophesies," and the first of these came from an "anthropoligist." It was, "Men will shrink to a height of two feet in another 2 million years." This may have been thought not portentious enough, because there was also a prediction by a dermatologist (correctly spelled) that in a hundred years or so men and women would go through life bald, and one from an astronomer that in a billion years or so the earth would be dry. Here was a portentious outlook indeed, men and women, members of a species that had been bald for 999,999,900 years, and had been two feet tall for 998,988,026, either seriously dehydrated or long since removed to other planets. (Among the earth's animals the camel had survived, being able to get his nose under the portent.)

There remained the question of what bald men and women two feet tall would be wearing while the earth was going dry. Wallach's had the answer in portentious prophesies by a designer and a hair stylist. The hair stylist said that men and women would soon be wearing gold and silver wigs for formal occasions, and the designer thought that reversible clothing might come in, so that a man could arrive at work wearing a gray worsted and, by turning it inside out, leave in a black dinner jacket. Here is the complete portentious outlook: bald men, two feet tall, wearing reversible thirty-four and thirty-six shorts for the most part, and bald women, two feet tall, wearing reversible dresses or pants suits bought from boutiques called Pocket Venus and Short Gals, while the earth turns into a desert littered with gold and silver wigs glinting in the relentless sunlight. Portentious isn't the word for it.

Most business language is not so evocative. It is simply wrong. Gulf Oil used to speak of "one of the most unique roadways ever built," which of course helped Gulf to be ready for what it so long claimed to be ready for — "Whatever the work there is to be done." TWA has long had it Amarillio, not Amarillo, Texas; B. Altman in New York advertises sweaters that are "definitly for a young junior"; Bergdorf Goodman makes it known that "an outstanding selection of luxurious furs are now available at tremendous reductions"; Cartier believes that a memorandum pad, a stationary holder, and a pencil cup make a triumverate; the Great Lakes Mink Association wrote a letter to a New York store, the Tailored Woman, referring to its "clientel," and the Tailored Woman was happy to print it in an advertisement, though I do not say that this is what caused the Tailored Woman to close down; the chain of men's stores, Broadstreet's, capitalizing on the growing interest in food, tried to sell some of its wares by spreading the word that "Good taste is creme sengelese soup in a mock turtleneck shirt from Broadstreet's," but the number of people in New York familiar with, or curious about, sengelese cooking must have been small, and even the later announcement, "We shrunk the prices on our premium men's stretch hose," did not keep Broadstreet's from disappearing from the New York scene. Hunting World, a New York shop, sells Ella Phant, "pride and joy of the Phant family," and says, "She's only 9" tall, and every little people you know will love her and you will too." Perhaps that depends on the kind of little people you know. Every little people that some of us know probably would be more interested in the Selig Imperial Oval Sofa, advertised by the Selig Manufacturing Company of Leominster, Massachusetts, which noted that "an orgy of 18 pillows, all shapes and colors, make a self-contained environment." An orgy do a lot of other things also.

Business language takes many forms. Camaraderie: "Us Tareyton smokers

would rather fight than switch."
Pomposity: When Morgan Guaranty Trust announced that negotiable securities worth $13,000,000 were missing from its vaults, it said, "A thorough preliminary search for the securities has been made, and a further search is now being made." All it needed to say was, "We're looking for them" — if indeed it couldn't expect its distinguished clients to take for granted that it was looking.

Pseudo science: "You are about to try the most technologically advanced shaving edge you can buy. Wilkinson Sword, with a world-wide reputation for innovation, brings you still another advance in razor blade technology, the first third-generation stainless steel blade. First, a microscopically thin layer of pure chromium is applied to the finely ground and stropped edge. Then, another layer of a specially developed chromium compound is applied. This special layer of chromium compound adds extra qualities of hardness, durability and corrosion resistance. Finally, a thin polymer film is coated onto the edge. This coating allows the blade to glide smoothly and comfortably over your face." Shaving seems an inadequate employment for so distinguished a product of razor blade technology, but even technology cannot hold back the dawn, and the razor is going the way of the reaper and the cotton gin. We are now invited to use the Trac-2 shaving system, which apparently is to the razor as the weapons system is to the bow and arrow. Much more of this might make you want to use the first third-generation stainless steel blade, or even the Trac-2, to slit your throat.

Stainless steel I may not be, but I was the first third-generation American in my family, on either trac, to hear life jackets carried on airliners referred to as articles of comfort. It was on a flight from London to New York in 1966, and the stewardess began her little lecture by saying, "Because of our interest in your comfort, we will now demonstrate your life jackets." It was a wonderful notion, classifying the gadget to be used after a plane has gone down in the North Atlantic as part of the comfort of flying.

Euphemistic business language can go no further. Only calling used cars pre-owned has, in my experience, equaled it.

The life jacket incident might have appealed to the novelist Evelyn Waugh. Waugh hated the modern world and wished that he had been born two or three centuries sooner, and he hated modern devices of transport and communication such as the automobile, which he refused to drive, and the airplane (about which more later), and the typewriter and the telephone, both of which he refused to use. This attitude was sometimes inconvenient. A new and lucrative British literary prize was about to be awarded at the time I met him, and he had some hope of getting it, and every time the telephone rang he had to wait for whichever member of the household was willing to have truck with it to tell him whether the hoped-for call had come. It never did.

In any case, in 1956 I made a short film with Waugh, for NBC, about the way he lived and the way he worked. I learned, among other things, that he wrote with a quill pen and professed to believe that

American reporters could not function without frequent infusions of whisky and that all Americans had been dye-vorced (his pronunciation) at least once.

We did the filming at his house — actually, it was a house provided by his father-in-law — in Stinchcombe, Gloucestershire. He had there a number of paintings he had collected, including a series of four called *The Pleasures of Travel.* Three were nineteenth-century paintings about the various discomforts of going by stagecoach, ship, and train. The fourth, which Waugh himself had commissioned, showed an airliner with a wing on fire. The passengers had been having breakfast, and they and their orange juice were being thrown all over the cabin as the aircraft plunged to destruction.

The other members of the NBC crew and I were frequent air travelers, and we all laughed hollowly for Waugh's benefit, as I also laughed hollowly on hearing the life jacket described as an article of comfort.

When we left at the end of the day a

couple of us asked Waugh to autograph books of his that we had brought along. I had *Officers and Gentlemen,* which had just come out. Waugh, who clearly had never taken a course in psychodynamic salesmanship or human engineering, made an ungracious remark about people who received free copies of books. I said that I had bought mine. He then wrote on the flyleaf, "To Edwin Newman (who bought it!)," and below that, "Souvenir of Stinchcombe," with his name and the date. I was unable to make out Souvenir and asked him what it was.

"Souvenir," he said. "That's French for remembrance."

Remembrance, with its touch of sentiment, is the kind of word much used in the women's beauty industry, which employs the most complex of the business tongues. Consider the following:

"The poets talk about lips that are warm, soft and moist.

"Most cosmetic ads talk about lips that are Ravishing Red or Pizzicato Pink.

"We think women ought to pay more attention to the poets than to the ads.

"That's why Germaine Monteil created Acti-Vita Emollient Lipstick."

Now take Princess Marcella Borghese, who promised an iridescent gloss of pearlized blushing color in Apricot Shimmer, Copper Shimmer, and Rose Shimmer. A woman's crowning glory is known to be her iridescent pearlized copper shimmer gloss, but this lacks the artful combination of moods and suggestions of Germaine Monteil — love (warm, soft, and moist) and the laboratory (Acti-Vita Emollient), seduction and science, the rapturous and the pharmaceutical.

The women's clothing industry also must tempt and reassure at the same time:

"Some of us just can't jump into those clingy new clothes and come off looking like they were made for us. We need the right kind of help in the right kind of places." The help is provided by a body briefer from Natural Smoothie. It is a garment in direct conflict with the principle of the legitimacy of multiple body styles, referred to earlier, but there are also multiple style styles.

Advertising aimed at women must of course keep up with the drive for equal rights. In the 1930s and 1940s the only acceptable female response to a cigar was an infatuation crossing over into insanity with the man who smoked one. Later, a woman sitting next to the man she loved — loved, as already noted, because he smoked cigars — was permitted to drool and simper because she wanted a stogie herself, and at a time when there was no national consensus on whether a gentleman should offer a Tiparillo to a lady.

Soon thereafter the Cigar Institute, which studies these things, estimated that there were sixty thousand female cigar smokers in the United States, many of whom belonged to cigar-smoking clubs in which they sat around and puffed away and, one supposes, cursed Fidel Castro. The latest estimate of those for whom having a cigarette of their own now, baby, and coming a long, long way is not enough is more than five hundred thousand. And the president of the Cigar Institute of

America, presumably for esthetic reasons, has come out against women smoking in the street, and not a moment too soon.

For other advertisers the best approach is the most direct. Thus Mitchum Anti-Perspirant's "Plan tonight to sweat less tomorrow." A corporate decision probably had to be made at the highest level not to say perspire, just as somebody must have authorized Winston cigarettes to taste good like rather than as, and somebody in a command role at Eastern Airlines, eyes teary with gratitude, must have said an eager "Yes" to "You gotta believe." That is how civilization moves ahead, through the pioneering of the visionary and the brave.

The national preoccupation with fetid armpits — and the profits therefrom; it's a $475,000,000-a-year business — suggest that had the product been available at the time, the Minutemen at Lexington and Concord and the other heroes of the American Revolution would have kept their antiperspirant, like their powder, dry, and that when the village smith's brow was wet with honest sweat, it was only because he was a boor and didn't mind offending others. With such an outlook Winston Churchill, who after all had an American mother, might have said, "I have nothing to offer but blood, toil, tears and antiperspirant."

The precursor of antiperspirants was Lifebuoy Soap, which shielded those who used it from B.O., which stood for Body Odor and was so dreadful an affliction that it has been spoken of only in initials, like V.D. and TB. It threatened the well-being of the nation at the same time that a number of manifestations of osis did. These were halitosis, which was fearlessly translated as bad breath; lordosis, too large a bottom, curable by corset; homitosis, which was bad taste in home furnishing; and gaposis, which meant that your clothes didn't fit as well or adjust as they should have because they did not have a certain brand of zipper. It had nothing to do with the dollar gap, and the credibility gap, and all of the other gaps that came along in various connections later on.

The nation survived B.O. and halitosis and such later dangers as tattletale gray, denture breath, morning mouth, unsightly bulge, and ring around the collar, only to find itself still, anticlimactically, perspiring.

When business turns its attention from customers to shareholders, the change in tone is drastic. Customers must be tempted and/or bullied; shareholders must be impressed and intimidated, wherefore the annual corporate reports. Something like six or seven thousand of these are issued every year, but the language is so nearly uniform that they may all be written by a single team, as paperback pornographic novels are written wholesale in porno novel factories. (I was about to say sweatshops, but I assume that for reasons already made clear, the sweatshop either is no more or exists only where perverseness bordering on un-Americanism lingers on.)

In the pornos, what counts is the detailed description of sexual enterprise. In corporate reports it is growth, which at the very least should be significant, and with any luck at all will be substantial. The ultimate for growth is to be dynamic. Whether it is, and whether it occurs at all, depends largely on growth opportunities; if they occur often enough, a consistent growth pattern may be achieved, brought about, perhaps, by an upward impetus that makes things move not merely fast but at an accelerated rate.

No company can grow, of course, without having a growth potential. To realize that potential, the company must have capabilities: overall capabilities, systems capabilities, flexible capabilities, possibly nuclear services capabilities, generating capabilities, environmental control capabilities, predictability capabilities. If all of these are what they should be, and the company's vitality, viability, and critical reliability are what *they* should be, the growth potential will be realized, and profitability should result.

There are, however, other factors that must mesh. Outlooks, solutions, and systems must be sophisticated, or, if possible, highly sophisticated or optimal.

Innovative products are requisite; they, in turn, are the consequence of innovative leadership that keeps its eye firmly on target areas, on inputs and outputs, on components and segments and configurations. Innovative leadership does this because capabilities are interrelated so that requirements, unwatched, may burgeon. For example, after a corporation has identified the objective of getting a new facility into start-up, environmental-impact reporting requirements must be met so that the facility can go on-stream within the envisaged time-span.

Even this tells only the bare bones of the story. Multiple markets and multi-target areas may well be penetrated, but not without impact studies, market strategies, cost economies, product development and product packaging, and consumer acceptance. Product packaging sounds simple enough, but it may call for in-house box-making capability. Box-making in turn is a process; that calls for process equipment capability; and *that* calls for process development personnel.

If all this is to be done, management teams must be sound and prudent and characterized by vision, enterprise, and flexibility. In a surprising number of companies, the corporate reports assure us, management teams are.

Business puts enormous pressure on language as most of us have known it. Under this pressure, triple and quadruple phrases come into being — high retention characteristics, process knowledge rate development, anti-dilutive common stock equivalents. Under this pressure also, adjectives become adverbs; nouns become adjectives; prepositions disappear; compounds abound.

In its report on 1972, American Buildings Company told its shareholders that its new products included "improved long-span and architectural panel configurations which enhance appearance and improve weatherability." Despite the travail concealed behind those simple words, the achievement must have been noteworthy on the cutting edge of the construction industry.

A statement by the Allegheny Power

System was, on the other hand, hardly worth making: "In the last analysis the former, or front-end, process seems the more desirable because the latter, or back-end, process is likely to create its own environmental problems." This is an old story, for the front-end process often does not know what the back-end process is doing.

In its annual report for 1972, Continental Hair Products drove home two lessons. One was that "Depreciation and amortization of property, plant and equipment are provided on the straight-line and double declining balance methods at various rates calculated to extinguish the book values of the respective assets over their estimated useful lives."

Among Continental's shareholders, one suspects, sentimentalists still quixotically opposed to the extinguishing of book values may have forborne to cheer. But not the others, and they must have been roused to still greater enthusiasm by the outburst of corporate ecstasy which was the second point: "Continental has exercised a dynamic posture by first establishing a professional marketing program and utilizing that base to penetrate multi-markets.''

For myself, looking at this array of horrors, I forbear to cheer. People are forever quoting Benjamin Franklin, coming out of the Constitutional Convention in 1776, being asked what kind of government the Convention was giving the country, and replying, ''A republic — if you can keep it.'' We were also given a language, and there is a competition in throwing it away. Business is in the competition and doing nicely. In its favor, however, one must note that business lags far behind the leader in throwing away the language we were bequeathed. The leader, moving confidently and without strain, is the social sciences. It is in the social sciences that the true language viability destruction-generating capacity lies.

In the summer and fall of 1951 I worked for three months in Greece for the Marshall Plan, under which the United States helped to bring about economic recovery in Western Europe after the

Second World War by providing billions of dollars of assistance in money, capital equipment, and technical advice. My job was to write stories about what was being accomplished in Greece, with the hope that these would be published in American newspapers, a hope only skimpily realized.

The resources of American social science were sometimes called in to help, and I remember seeing a report on how to reach the Turkish peasant, it being thought that this might help us to reach the Greek. The Turkish peasant had no radio (television was not yet a factor), he could not read, and he had no access to moving-picture theaters. The solution, arrived at after research and analysis, and possibly amid cries of "Eureka," was a van that would carry information films, a projector, and a screen on which to show them.

In Greece, an American university's applied social science research team examined the way opinion was formed in the villages and brought forth a concept and three subcategories. The team found that the priest, the schoolteacher, and the mayor were usually the only ones in the village who could read, and designated them opinion leaders. The rest of the population was designated opinion followers. However, the taverna in each village usually had a radio, to which people listened, and the taverna proprietor had the power to switch the radio on and off and to twirl the dial. Taverna owners were therefore designated opinion controllers.

That was one of my early experiences with academic jargon. There have been many since, including, most recently, a series of surveys of cultural trends said to be transforming the American work ethic. The surveys found that those people most likely to be dissatisfied with their work were "By and large . . . those under 35, those who have high expectations of what their jobs will offer and those who seek psychological rewards from their jobs." The full implications of this finding, that those who wanted and expected most felt the greatest disappointment, may not be understood for some time.

The ability to use jargon is learned at an increasingly early age. From February 23 to 27, 1974, an organization called the National Student Lobby held its third annual conference. It took place at the Thomas Circle - Ramada Inn in Washington, D. C., and it seems to have been pretty much a prearranged affair, to judge by a press release received a few days before it began.

"Students To Site Grievances at National Conference," the press release was headed, thereby suggesting that the students in the National Students Lobby might be wise to lobby for courses in spelling if, as appears, it is not part of their curriculums. The alternative was to believe that these were grievances gathered from their usual locations, roughly midway between the liberal arts faculty parking lot and the Office of Course Relevance Certification, and placed so as to remain stationary at the Thomas Circle - Ramada Inn for some time to come. Students' grievances are not very cheerful to have around, but the Thomas Circle - Ramada Inn probably had no convention groups due in later that needed space for grievances of their own.

The same press release had Arthur Rodbell, executive director of NSL, saying, "A unique feature of this year's conference will consist of 'role playing' sessions in which six members of Congress will participate.

"In the first phase of these sessions," the press release went on, "students will practice their lobbying techniques on these Congresspersons, who will assume their normal roles. During the second phase, the members will switch roles: students will assume the Congressperson's role and the Congressperson's that of the students."

The press release then went back to quoting Rodbell: " 'This will help prepare the students for actual lobbying in pursuant days on Capitol Hill,' Rodbell commented."

After noting that the apostrophe in the second Congressperson's above has no business there and would go on having none even in pursuant days, one supposes that the students doing genuine lobbying in pursuant days would stay away from the congresspersons they were practicing with, since these congresspersons would surely spot the rehearsed techniques and discount them.

In pursuant days in New York City, where grievances are often sited, the objection was made by a union official that some Spanish-speaking school principals chosen by community boards could barely read or write English. The chancellor of the city's schools, Irving Anker, rose to the occasion with a notable example of candor and concrete expression. Among "some of the new supervisors," he said, "there may be a lesser demonstration of formal academic standards."

At about the same time, a letter arrived on my desk from the director of the Office of Information Services at Dartmouth College that offered a greater demonstration of formal academic standards. I have no wish to embarrass Dartmouth College, assuming that to be possible, but the letter is representative of much of the language coming out of academe these days, and something must be done to try to stop it. The director wrote about a press conference that was to be held to announce the results of a two-year study by nine eastern private universities and colleges of the financing of higher education. The nine institutions were described as a "diverse leadership group of schools" forming themselves into an "on-going consortium" as a by-product of the study.

A summary of the report and a press release were enclosed for my "prior background information," and I was told that the report contained "arresting conclusions of almost watershed quality," but no "easy panaceas," or hard ones either, I suppose. The letter concluded, "Looking forward to hopefully seeing you."

There may be something in the air in New England. In June, 1974, Hampshire College in South Amherst, Massachusetts, graduated its first class. The plans for the college were set out in December, 1966, as a "working paper," and so far as I know, the language has never been equaled.

These were some of the positions taken: that social structure should optimally be the consonant patterned expression of culture; that higher education is enmeshed in a congeries of social and political change; that the field of the humanities suffers from a surfeit of leeching, its blood drawn out by verbalism, explication of text, Alexandrian scholiasticism, and the exquisite preciosities and pretentiousness of contemporary literary criticism; that a formal curriculum of acadamic substance and sequence should not be expected to contain mirabilia which will bring all the educative ends of the college to pass, and that any formal curriculum should contain a high frangibility factor; that the College hopes that the Hampshire student will have kept within him news of Hampshire's belief that individual man's honorable choice is not between immolation in a senseless society or withdrawal into the autarchic self but instead trusts that his studies and experience in the College will confirm for him the choice that only education allows:

detachment and skill enough to know, engagement enough to feel, and concern enough to act, with self and society in productive interplay, separate and together; that an overzealous independence reduces linguistics to a kind of cryptographic taxonomy of linguistic forms, and that the conjoining of other disciplines and traditional linguistics becomes most crucial as problems of meaning are faced in natural language; and that the College expects its students to wrestle most with questions of the human condition, which are, What does it mean to be human? How can men become more human? What are human beings for?

Readers are encouraged to turn back and read that again. I'll be happy to wait before pushing on to the bluff and earthier Middle West.

I once made a speech under the auspices of the Educational Facilities Center in Chicago, an organization dedicated to improving teaching in primary schools, junior high schools, and high schools. From the program of the meeting I drew the following:

"Overview." What one of the speakers was offering.

"Authored." What one of the speakers had done to a book. If authored, why not authoring? Why not, "He playwrighted a play," and "She paintered a picture"?

"Select the sessions of your choice," in preference, apparently, to selecting the sessions of somebody else's.

Also:

"She is a member of a Junior High Humanities Team which employs an interdisciplinary process approach to education."

"Probed in this session will be what goes on between the teacher and child, showing the relativeness of communication skills."

"Participants will explore the concepts of communication, expressive arts and language skills, the technique of individualizing, and the place of language arts in the developmental stages of a total person. Dr. DuFault" (Nap DuFault, principal of Westmont High School, Westmont, Illinois, and professor of education at Illinois Benedictine College) "will treat both the philosophical as well as the practical day-to-day needs of preparing students for power through communications."

We may ignore the minor error in grammar in "both the philosophical as well as the practical." We may acknowledge — I certainly do, from what I saw — that these are good, worthy, and devoted people engaged in valuable work. I have no reason to doubt that this is true at Dartmouth and the other eight diverse leadership institutions as well. They do, however, reflect influences brought to bear on them for at least a couple of decades, and they are influential themselves. They have helped to carry us into a world in which speaking and writing have become communication skills, in which on-going consortia work out interdisciplinary approaches and people look forward to hopefully seeing each other, and in which the module is all. It is a world in which things that are good for society are positive externalities and things that are bad are negative externalities, in which unemployment is classified as an adverse social consequence, in which subjects are listed under rubrics rather than headings, rationing becomes end-use allocation, stressful situations arise in the nuclear or matrifocal family, and people in minigroups or, if the shoe fits, maxigroups are in a state of cognitive inertia because self-actualization is lacking.

The Committee for the Future, Inc., which describes itself as a non-profit, tax-exempt educational organization, proclaims that its purpose "is to discover, articulate and bring new options for a positive future into the arena of public discussion for action." When, as part of its process of public participation and planning, known as synergistic convergence, it brings together "leaders and pioneers — builders of new options for humanity," it serves them conviviality at seven o'clock and dinner at eight. Dinner is an old option, and so is conviviality, but in a new guise:

In some secluded rendezvous,
That overlooks the avenue,
With someone sharing a delightful chat
Of this and that,
And conviviality for two.

I think it may be better to grunt unintelligibly than to use such language, for it is so impersonal and manufactured as to be almost inhuman. Not that there is any mystery about why it is used. Social science jargon is tempting because it sounds weighty, important, rather like the policeman's ''I observed the perpetrator,'' followed, all being well, by ''I apprehended the perpetrator.'' The Iowa chapter of the National Agri-Marketing Association recently called my attention to Iowa Agriculture Day. The letter was signed by the chairman of its Media-Awareness Committee. The jargon is catching, too. I work with a man who ordinarily speaks well and plainly, and sometimes with passion. When a program brought in letters from the State Department and two United States senators, he wrote me that we had achieved "penetration of significant audience strata."

At that, penetration of significant audience strata was child's play compared with what was recently visited on parents of children in the lower grades of the public schools in Dallas. Instead of report cards, they received coded reports, and to help them understand the code, a manual, twenty-eight pages long, called "Terminal Behavior Objectives for Continuous Progression Modules in Early Childhood Education." Later, a local advertising man was hired to simplify the manual and make it shorter.

A large part of social scientific practice consists of taking clear ideas and making them opaque. Carl W. Hale and Joe Walters showed their peer group the way in "Appalachian Regional Development and the Distribution of Highway Benefits": "It is thus probable that . . . highway development expenditures will conform de facto to the efficiency criterion, and will have their greatest initial impact on the periphery of Appalachia, where the more viable growth centers are located." Which is to say, money to build highways in Appalachia probably will be spent where it will do the most good, and at first in the growing towns on the edge of the region.

Lee Rainwater was quoted by Daniel P. Moynihan, a member of his peer group, in *On Understanding Poverty:* "The social ontogeny of each generation recapitulates the social phylogeny of Negroes in the New World *because the basic socioeconomic position of the group has not changed in a direction favorable to successful achievement in terms of conventional norms."* Or each generation of American Negroes, like its predecessors, makes less money than whites.

For a social scientist to make obscure what he considers to be unnecessarily clear calls not so much for an imagination as for an appropriate vocabulary in which boundaries are parameters, parts are components, things are not equal but co-equal, signs are indicators, and causes are dependent or exogenous variables (and it may take a regression analysis to find out which). To know oneself is to have self-awareness, communities being studied are target areas, thinking is conceptualization, patterns are configurations, and people do not speak but articulate or verbalize; nor are they injured: they are traumatized.

The jargon may, on rare occasions, take on a vigorous flavor, so that you hear of imperatives and of dynamic hypotheses. Usually, however, the words are leaden — archetypal, misspecification, disaggregates.

Once you've caught on to the technique, it's easy. For example, in the social sciences as in business language, inputs and outputs are everywhere. You do it this way: In a school, textbooks and students and faculty-student ratios are inputs; so are chalk and basketballs. Good citizenship and reading scores are outputs.

You can move on quickly to more complex constructions. Siblings are conflicted in their interpersonal relationships means that children of the same parent or parents don't like each other. Exogenous variables form the causal linkage that explains the poverty impact, the behavior modification, and the intergroup dissonance in the target area means that outside factors cause the poverty and the changes in people that lead to trouble in the neighborhood. A recommendation by a medical ethicist that a physician obtain an input from the patient's own value system means that the patient should be asked whether he wants the treatment.

These are, I confess, pushovers, and they leave us with healthy reserves, including the two all-purpose whizbangs, role reversal and interstitial. Versatile as these are, they should not be squandered. Role reversal and interstitial should be used when nothing else is available and the situation is desperate.

Luckily for those who give money to the various claimants (an act known as funding; with foundation offices in the buildings that tower over the harbor, New York is the Bay of Funding), there is a certain comity in the social sciences. Suppose, however, that the money ran short and the various centers and institutes saw their existence endangered? All would refuse to self-destruct and a great jurisdictional dispute would set in over the precious lifeblood that enables all of them to measure cumulative impact, which, next to things coming together in the state known as inter, is the greatest problem facing society today. Who would win, among the centers and institutes, the academies, projects and programs for Contemporary Problems, Society, Ethics, and the Life Sciences, Mental Health Research, Behavior Modification, Study of Democratic Institutions, Study of the Person, Child Study, Interracial Justice, Faith and Order, Critical Choices, Policy Alternatives, Policy Research, Human Relations, Inter-American Relations, and the rest?

Some might make a better case than others, but suppose they all said they wanted to set up ongoing ad hoc mechanisms for option assessment and constructive and creative response? Suppose they all wanted to draft programmatic proposals that could later be implemented on the basis of a meaningful ethos able to supply definitive answers to fundamental value questions and identify dangerous fallout? Suppose — the ultimate horror — they all claimed not only the same set of concerns but the same constituency within which an informed dialogue would resonate? What price cross-fertilization at the interface then?

One thinks of priceless bits of natural eloquence, remembered for years. There was the boy in the West Indies who offered me a shoeshine. I said no thanks. "All right," said he, a resourceful salesman, "how about a dus' off?"

I remember the concern of a porter in a New York apartment building about a pothole in the street. "A person," he said, "could break their bot' arms."

My own father, when he could tolerate his school-age sons no longer, would fire a warning shot across our bows. "I'll hit you so hard," he would say, "you won't know where it came from." As a behavioral psychologist would say, it provided reinforcement.

On the other hand, Abraham Lincoln was on the side of the social scientists when he said, "God must have loved the people of lower and middle socio-economic status, because he made such a multiplicity of them."

6

Is Your Team Hungry Enough, Coach?

Meaning no disrespect, I suppose there is, if not general rejoicing, at least a sense of relief when the football season ends. It's a long season.

I have an additional reason for watching football fade out without much regret. That reason is a protective interest in the English language. The phrase "pretty good," as in "He hit him pretty good," and "We stopped them pretty good," and "He moves pretty good for a big man," gets worked out pretty good from late September to mid-January. After which it should be given a pretty good rest, or allowed to rest pretty good, or at any rate left to basketball, where they hit the backboards pretty good.

Basketball, of course, cannot be played without referees, and generally they do the officiating pretty good, but not always. Said K. C. Jones, coach of the Capital Bullets of the NBA, explaining why he would not comment on the officiating in a play-off game against New York: "No sense in risking a $2,000 fine. To hell with it. They read the papers pretty good for our remarks."

After basketball, baseball. Al Downing of the Los Angeles Dodgers, who threw home run number 715 to Henry Aaron: "I was trying to get it down to him, but I didn't and he hit it good — as he would. When he first hit it, I didn't think it might be going. But like a great hitter, when he picks his pitch, chances are he's going to hit it pretty good."

Pretty good has its final flowering in football on the Sunday of the Superbowl, when opinion is likely to be general that one reason the winners beat the losers was that they stopped their running game pretty good. The losers might have been able to make up for this even though they were hurting pretty good, meaning that some of their players were injured, if they had got their passing game going pretty good, but they didn't, and that was that: the winners were the world champions.

When the majestic ocean liner the *QE 2* tossed gently in the balmy Atlantic, her engines dead, early in April, 1974, a number of American football players and coaches were aboard, showing films and giving chalk talks as part of the entertainment. One was Hank Stram, coach of the Kansas City Chiefs. Stram told a reporter that after emergency repairs the ship had "moved along pretty good" for thirty minutes. It is necessary to stay in shape during the off-season.

At the 1974 Superbowl, Pat Summerall, in search of a more analytical explanation, attributed the success of the Miami Dolphins' defense to their having "so many different variations," leaving us to suppose that the Minnesota Vikings' defense failed because their variations were uniform. Ray Scott, working with

Summerall, told us that Larry Csonka "apparently is injured around his one eye." He may have had Csonka confused with the legendary fullback Cyclops, who helped the Giants defeat the Titans but, unlike Csonka, never played on a world championship team.

World champions — there's another point. Are they really? They are the champions of the National Football League, but they have not played any teams in other leagues. No doubt they could beat them — the others are minor leagues, after all — but that still would not make them world champions. American football is not played in other countries, and it is a little hard to be world champion in a game that is played in your country only. It is as though a Siamese claimed to be world champion in boxing Thai-style, or a Scotsman claimed to be world champion in tossing the caber. World championships require some international competition, and in American-style football there isn't any.

The same is true of the baseball World Series. It may be a series, but it is grandiose to speak of the world. Perhaps it is a harmless conceit, but the American and National leagues do not represent the world, even with two divisions each and a team in Montreal.

The teams aren't usually very good, either. In these days talent is spread so thin by expansion that some players doing regular duty swagger up to the plate with .189 batting averages and nobody thinks there is anything untoward about it. These players are often said to have a way of coming through with timely hits. When you're batting .189, any hit you get is likely to be timely.

Still, whether the World Series is played is determined not by the quality of the teams but by the annual occurrence of October, and again, whatever the quality of the teams, the series must end in seven games or less, which is the sports-page version of seven games or fewer. Equally inescapable is the pre-series analysis, in which the experts, paid and unpaid, compare the opposing sides, weigh their strengths and weaknesses, evaluate their physical condition, take note of the weather, calculate which side has more of that magical substance, momentum, and point out that the breaks can nullify any advantage, that anything can happen in a short series, and that you still have to win them one at a time.*

In this arcane atmosphere you may find yourself reading an explanation of why, although Team A's first baseman hits better with men on than Team B's does, Team B's first baseman has more rbis. The explanation is that the man with more rbis (runs batted in, or ribbies to the cognoscenti) had more chances to bat in runs because he came up fourth in the order whereas the other came up sixth. However, the man who batted sixth might have done better had he been allowed to bat in the cleanup position, and indeed he wanted to but allowed himself to be placed in the sixth position for the higher good of the team and an interest-free loan from the club owner.

Even for the most knowing,

---

* In boxing there is a rough equivalent of this: They both only got two hands.

comparisons are difficult in a time when a manager may platoon left field with four players of different sizes, depending on the height of the outfield grass, but once the experts' analyses are complete, they interview the managers. The answers are purely ritualistic, but nobody minds. It is part of the great fall classic. I will omit the questions and give only the answers.

"Getting runs home is the name of the game, and my boys have shown all year that they can get the runs home."

"Pitching is the name of the game, and we have the pitching."

"I think our rookies will do pretty good."

"I think our veterans will do pretty good. Their records speak for themselves."

"The double play is the name of the game, and our guys can really turn it over."

"Hustle is the name of the game, and nobody is going to outhustle us."

"Pride is the name of the game, and we didn't come this far to lose."

"Kirilenko closed with a rush this

season and got his average up to .219, and I look for some real power hitting from him."

"Frelinghuysen has good speed and good power. But we think we can handle him."

"Yes, I think so." (I'd better give the question here. It was "Do you think you can put it all together?")

Putting it all together was identified as the key to success a few years ago, and it has swept all other explanations before it. When the series has ended, it accounts for one team's coming out with the right to fly the championship flag while the other does not. Many things go into putting it all together: pitchers reach back and give it everything they've got; infielders go skyward after errant throws; pivot men in twin killings elude sliding runners (nobody has come up with a synonym for slide); outfielders swing potent bats and scamper to the farthermost barrier to haul in arching blasts, while on the side that did not put it all together outfielders also scamper to the farthermost barrier to haul in arching blasts but swing once-potent bats, now shackled; bloopers barely escape desperate grasps; balls are deposited in the distant seats; heady days of glory are relived; speed on the base paths pays off; somebody trots out his assortment of breaking pitches, to his opponents' almost total frustration; and it is found once more that there is no substitute for the high hard one when the high hard one is needed. And, when starters get into trouble, relief pitchers warm up and the announcers tell us, "There is activity in the bullpen." Ogden Nash once wrote a poem about a relief pitcher named MacTivity so that he could say, "There is MacTivity in the bullpen."

The interview before World Series closely resembles the spring training season interview. Again it is a two-character affair. The sports writer is named Buck and the manager is named Al. Buck's first question is, "Well, Al, how do you think you'll do this year?" Al is not thrown by this. He says, "Well, I think we'll do pretty good. I think we'll do all right."

Buck follows that up like a hawk. He

says, a shade aggressively, "Well, are you predicting the pennant, Al?" Al replies that well, they won it last year, and the other teams are going to have to beat them. He knows one thing: they are not going to beat themselves.

The interview has been under way for about a minute at this point, and nobody has said anything about the name of the game. This is now remedied. Buck asks Al where he thinks his main strength lies, and Al replies that scoring runs is the name of the game and his boys can get the runs home. Buck then says that some people think pitching is the name of the game, and Al says it is, it is, and he thinks his pitchers will do pretty good, but he still has one outstanding need, a reliever who can go at top speed for a full inning without tiring. He has such a man on the roster, a Cuban named Felix Miguel Arbanzas Lopez y Puesto, a real flame thrower, but there is some question about Castro's letting him out and the FBI's letting him in.

Buck asks about right field, normally occupied by High Pockets Kirilenko, a somewhat moody player who (as we know) closed with a rush last season and got his average up to .219. Al says that Kirilenko has good speed and good power, but because of that big .219 average Kirilenko is holding out for a share of the concession revenue, a commitment by the club owner to cover any losses he may sustain on his investments in the stock market, and the services of a hairdresser before each game.

If High Pockets doesn't get in line, Al will try the French Canadian rookie, Willie LaBatt. LaBatt has been up before, but he really shattered the fences in the Australian Instructional League over the winter, and he may be ready. Al also has hopes for his new first baseman, Cy (The Eel) Lamprey, who should be a ballplayer because he grew up in the shadow of Ebbets Field. In fact, Lamprey was lost briefly under the debris when they tore it down, but they dug him out and he looks pretty good.

The team will, however, miss second baseman Ron Larrabee, who had so much range to his left that he crashed into the first-base stands going after a grounder and broke his shoulder at a crucial juncture of last year's pennant race. Larrabee is therefore hobbled by injuries and not yet ready.

The interview is approaching its climax. Soon fielding is the name of the game, and so is base running. Buck's last question is whether pride isn't really the name of the game, and whether Al, who has pride, can communicate it to his players. Al replies that if he didn't think he could, he wouldn't be there, and while you never know in baseball, his team has a real good shot. Buck says, "You better believe it," and there, to the regret of all, the interview ends.

There is an alternative ending, more appropriate in some cases — for example, in Al's, since his team made it into the series last year. It is:

"Is your team hungry enough, Al?"

"I don't think a team can ever be hungry enough."

Regional differences in speech are easily accommodated by this last exchange:

"Is your team hongry enough, coach?"

"I don't think a team can ever be hongry enough."

In the closing days of the 1973 baseball season, I watched on television a game between the Pittsburgh Pirates and the Montreal Expos that was delayed by rain several times and for a total of more than three hours. At one point the play-by-play announcer, Jim Simpson, remarked that it was "raining pretty good." He must have been embarrassed because he immediately added, "It's raining pretty hard."

There is no way to measure the destructive effect of sports broadcasting on ordinary American English, but it must be considerable. In the early days sports broadcasting was done, with occasional exceptions such as Clem McCarthy, by non-experts, announcers. Their knowledge of the sports they described varied, but their English was generally of a high order. If they could not tell you much about the inside of the game they were covering, at any rate what they did tell you you could understand.

Then came the experts, which is to say the former athletes. They could tell you a great deal about the inside, but — again with some exceptions — not in a comprehensible way. They knew the terms the athletes themselves used, and for a while that added color to the broadcasts. But the inside terms were few, and the nonathlete announcers allowed themselves to be hemmed in by them — "He got good wood on that one," "He got the big jump," "He really challenged him on that one," "They're high on him," "They came to play," "He's really got the good hands," and "That has to be," as in "That has to be the best game Oakland ever played."

The effect is deadening, on the enjoyment to be had from watching sports on television or reading about them, and since sports make up so large a part of American life and do so much to set its tone, on the language we see and hear around us.

There is one sports announcer who does not go where the former athletes lead him. That is Howard Cosell. Cosell is a phenomenon, or as some have it, phenomena. Nothing can shake him away from his own bromides, of which the supply is unquenchable. Cosell can range from a relative paucity ("Despite the relative paucity of scoring . . .") to a veritable plethora (Let's continue on this point of this veritable plethora of field goals") without drawing a breath, and there is every reason to believe that when he says "relative paucity" and "veritable plethora" he is not kidding; he means it.

Only Cosell would have described the mood of the crowd at the Bobby Riggs - Billie Jean King match as "an admixture" or remarked that for Riggs "It has not been a comedic night." Only Cosell would speak of a football team "procuring a first down," or say that a fighter was "plagued by minutiae," or that the cards of the referee and judges, made public after each round in a fight in Quebec, "vivified" the problem facing the fighter who was behind. During a Monday night football game nobody else would say, "The Redskins have had two scoring opportunities and failed to avail themselves both times," or that "The mist is drifting over the stadium like a description in the Thomas Hardy novel." At any rate, we may hope that nobody else would say it.

I am far from arguing that the language of athletes and former athletes never adds to the gaiety of the nation. Jake LaMotta, the old middleweight, interviewed long after his fighting days were over, told his questioner that he had no fear of the future because "I got too much growing for me." Another middleweight Rocky Graziano, during his fighting days was pleased with his reception in the Middle West. He said, "They trutt me right in Chicago." An old ballplayer, Joe Hauser, had the same sort of genius. Near the end of his career, badly slowed down, he was retired on what should have been a single to right. He said with some bitterness, "They trun me out at first."

Joe Jacobs, manager of the German heavyweight Max Schmeling in the 1930s, described his dreamlike condition when a decision unexpectedly went against his man: "I was in a transom." Before their first fight Joe Frazier said of Muhammad Ali, "He don't phrase me," and was right on both counts, and Ali spoke of not being "flustrated," which he rarely was. In one of the disputes over rules at the 1972 Olympics, a United States swimming coach spoke of signing "alphadavits." We would all be poorer without this.

Mention of disputes over rules carries me back to the annual fall classic. If a player is thumbed out, or given the heave-ho, by an umpire, the precedent is more than a century and a quarter old. This is on the authority of the New York Public Library, which was inspired to do the research after I spoke on television about the complaint by the former National League umpire Jocko Conlan against abuse of umpires by players and fans. Conlan wrote, "I don't understand why the fans boo an umpire. I know a lot of it is humorous, and it's part of the game, and the American way and all that. But why is it? Who started booing the umpire and calling him a blind bat and saying, 'Kill the ump!' "

The library could not answer the

question directly, but it did find out that the first player to be disciplined by an umpire was named Davis, and that he swore at the umpire and was fined six cents. This unpleasantness took place as soon as humanly possible, in the first game between organized teams, the New York Knickerbockers and the New York Club, on June 19, 1846. The scene was the Elysian Fields in Hoboken, New Jersey.

I look for the Boston Braves, or as they are also called, the Philadelphia Athletics, to take this year's fall classic in six.

Although I have spent a fair part of my life in Britain, British sports, unlike American sports, are of little interest to me. I am impressed by the sustained violence of rugby, and I can appreciate that cricket calls in a greater range of complexities than baseball does, but I think you have to grow up with a sport to have much feeling for it.

British sports writing, on the other hand, can be fascinating, for several reasons — the literary tradition, the naïveté, and the fact that the British almost never win anything in international competition, which means that the writers have to provide in the word the excitement that is missing in the deed.

I remember, for example, during the 1972 Olympics, a British expert describing a fight and saying of one of the fighters, "If he hits him hard again, he will be doing much better." Of another bout, the expert said that one of the boxers would be in trouble if he let the other man "get to him too often." These were what are now known as insightful remarks.

When the British champion Lynn Davies was eliminated from the Olympic long jump competition, the commentator explained that his last jump was of a kind that Davies "didn't really want to make." British commentators help their viewers to understand the situation in ways that Americans do not.

Similarly, during the 1500 meters, a British runner, Alan Foster, was lying fifth when the British commentator felt called upon to point out that Foster was "more aware than anyone of what he can do." The viewers must have found this good to know.

In one of the boxing finals, a Cuban against a Mexican, the commentator noted that the Cuban had defeated the British entry and was "now looking for similar success." Again the insight.

I went to Britain in 1949. I had not been there very long before there was a light-heavyweight fight between Joey Maxim of the United States and Freddie Mills of Britain. British sports writers showed great restraint. Only one wrote that it was a duel between the Maxim gun and the Mills bomb. He may, of course, have been the only one old enough to remember the weapons of the First World War.

This restraint fooled me, but I quickly learned that British sports writers could let themselves go, though in a way we would hardly expect.

The between-rounds man for the BBC in those days, radio days, was W. Barrington Dalby. He entered on the cue "Come in, Barry," and reached the peak of his career one night when he said that one of the fighters was "a better puncher qua puncher" than the other. So far as I know, this is the only time Latin has been invoked to explain the course of a fight.

It was at about the same time that a boxing writer for the *Daily Telegraph* wrote that one fighter's immense courage had enabled him "to give perhaps a quarter of a Roland for an Oliver." So far as I know, this is the only time the *Chanson de Roland* has been invoked to explain the course of a fight.

The Roland and Oliver swapping might have led one to believe that it was the *Telegraph* that was preeminent among British papers in having an Old World approach to sports. Not so. The *Times* of London is a paper that, in referring to a man who had been left more than £2,000,000, thought it a fair comment that he was "not endowed with the world's goods," and it once remarked editorially that "to plunge into a third world war would not be the best means of defending peace." This style spilled over into the sports pages, making the *Times* preeminent. It has since lost some of the old flair, but preeminent it still is.

You will appreciate why I speak of the *Times*'s old flair when I quote its pre-game story on the All-England soccer final in 1951. It begins plainly enough: The King and Queen will be there, the match is between Arsenal and Liverpool, it will be played in Wembley Stadium, it is the sixty-ninth such final. With that, however, the *Times* man is off:

"The teams will be birds of a strange plumage, indeed — Arsenal in shirts of old gold and white trimmings; Liverpool in white with red facings. But the disguises will in no way cloak the simple fact that once more the ritual of a Cup Final will have been set in motion."

Having reassured those who might have thought that the new colors meant that the Final would *not* be played, he continues:

"A crowd 100,000 strong will be ranged around the curving, elliptical basin of Wembley, its clear rim far up, cutting the sky. Yet beyond that, and beyond exact computation, some millions will be there in spirit, linked by radio and television with this scene; for the Cup Final, like the

Derby, the Grand National, and the Boat Race, is a sporting event of national interest that draws a whole people together."

Letting fly an "alas" — knowing precisely when to let one fly is among the most highly specialized techniques in all British writing — the *Times* man yearns for "Kennington Oval, first home of the competition, where once the crowds, removing the horses from the shafts of Lord Kinnaird's carriage, drew the great man in his vehicle to the entrance of the pavilion for one of his nine appearances in the early finals."

He admits, though, that Wembley also has its points: exquisite velvet turf, community singing, the solemn moments of "Abide with Me," the feeling for ritual, the controlled excitement. "Seldom," he writes, "has an afternoon passed there without its full share of dramatic upheaval."

By this time, perhaps, the reader could not be blamed for losing the thread. This the *Times* man is able to sense.

"Into this atmosphere," he notes

quickly, "now sharpened by a North v. South motif, will stride Arsenal, twice winners of the Cup, and Liverpool, who have yet to lay their hands on the trophy." Rather reluctantly, he then mentions the teams' records, their personnel and playing styles, and their chances.

I concluded that the man who wrote the story was about to retire and didn't care that he had left himself nothing for next year.

The *Times* golf correspondent was somewhat less spendthrift, but in the same vein:

"Walton Heath with a blue sky, a hot sun, and cooling northeasterly wind before which the young birches bowed their heads in their new green liveries — what better conditions could anyone desire for the watching of golf?" The question was rhetorical, and the story went on:

"This was the second day of the *Daily Mail* golf tournament, the end of which would see a sad chopping off of heads before the final two rounds on the third day."

Which heads were chopped off, which were not? Only the most pedestrian sports writer would tell. Instead: "As the hours wore on with comparatively few low scores, it seemed that Walton Heath had the better of the argument and the qualifying scores would be high."

Here there is a diversion to describe a round played by Alf Perry, and presently, in the thirty-third line, we are informed that Perry's two-round total was one forty-two, which gave him a two-stroke lead over Ward. On line 84 — after a detour in which the *Times* golf correspondent remarks that Ossie Pickworth of Australia was the man he most wanted to see and that he was not disappointed — we are told that Pickworth came in with a seventy-three and was only one stroke behind Perry. A good writer makes you feel that you were present. The *Times* man makes you feel that you played the round, carrying the clubs yourself, with rocks in the bag.

It is, naturally, in cricket, which has produced a vast literature of its own, that the literary allusion flourishes. Thus the

Times cricket correspondent from Sydney, Australia:

"Once more your messenger enters to report a setback. But not, be it noted, with the sickening self-satisfaction of his ancient Greek counterpart whose probably sole delight was to catch the King in a moment of rare happiness and to tell him with sadistic prolixity that his summer palace was burnt to the ground and that his mother, in whose continued existence the King still fondly believed, was even now crossing the River Styx, then to leave the bemused monarch to the beard-waggings and breast-beatings of an ancient and admonitory chorus.

"No, the chorus will be controlled. But the King will recover, perhaps within the week. He has done so before. In short, our cricketers out here are like many fighters of repute. They need to be knocked down first. It is partly a matter of temperament. Their performance against Queensland just before the first Test match was too bad to be real. It is hoped by Australian as well as English spectators that the same may be true of their current performance at Sydney. After two days of play, M.C.C., with three batsmen gone, are still 479 runs behind an Australian eleven's total.''

That, of course, is cricket. Could a boxing writer hope to measure up to that standard? Probably not. Still:

''Hopes and fears were nicely balanced in the chief contest at Harringay last night, with rather less intense feeling intermittently aroused by the efforts of the novices engaged in a heavyweight competition.''

So! The novices engaged in a heavyweight competition aroused only moderately intense feeling. Let us carry on:

''The interest in the two chief bouts also was nicely divided, though, in the titular sense, it was clearly more important that Terry Allen, the Islington flyweight, should win a world championship recently given up by Rinty Monaghan than that Danny O'Sullivan, the bantam champion of Great Britain, should acquire a European title as well.''

Having brushed aside O'Sullivan's

feelings in the matter, probably biased, the *Times* man has established the relative values of the two bouts. He continues:

"Both were confronted by sufficiently formidable foreign boxers, and Allen's opponent, Honoré Pratesi of France, had once outpointed him over ten rounds." Now he looses the dull fact: "This time, in a tiring rather than punishing fight, Allen won, and deserved to do so, on points."

This information digested, what of O'Sullivan? Granted that it was not so important for him to win, we might nonetheless be given a clue. That is not the way. There must be first a strictly chronological account of the Allen-Pratesi bout, covering five hundred and seventy-five words. Then:

"The fight between Danny O'Sullivan and Luis Romero of Spain, a southpaw with a devastating punch in either hand, had a hair-raising start. It remained hair-raising to round 13, when Romero was declared the winner." After three hundred words of another round-by-round account, there are two lines for the novices engaged in a heavyweight competition mentioned in what I would once have been unimaginative enough to refer to as the lead.

The main lesson to be learned from British sports writing in those days, two and more decades ago, was to suppress any inclination to unseemly haste. Here is a last example of how it is done, drawn from the *Sunday Times,* which was then unconnected, except in spirit, with the other *Times:*

"It being impossible even in this age of speed to be in two places at the same time, I devoted part of a perfect Saturday afternoon to the White City, and part to the Chiswick stadium.

"At the former," the story goes on, "the first London Caledonian games ever held in London provided food for all tastes. I confess with shame that I have never yet seen a Highland games meeting on its native heath. I intend to remedy the deficiency at the earliest opportunity. There was a most impressive opening ceremony, which did not seem in the least out of place, and the 'call to the gathering' made spectator, dancer, official and athlete alike feel that they were sharing in a common spectacle.''

Three more paragraphs — equally absorbing — follow, and then it comes: ''Later in the afternoon, E. MacDonald Bailey won the 220 yards in 21.1 seconds. If this time were to be recognized, which is unlikely, it would beat by one-tenth of a second the British record made by W. R. Applegarth in 1914.''

It is hard to resist the feeling that Bailey should be ashamed of himself for intruding. Getting that reaction from one's readers was, in those days, the ideal for which to strive.

All of that came, as noted, in the early 1950s. It has changed since then, but not entirely. I remember a Wimbledon in the middle 1950s in which the *Times*'s tennis man wrote of Frank Sedgman of Australia that he ''bestrode the court like a colossus.'' One might hesitate to use such language about a tennis match, but a dozen years later there was this, about the South African, Barry Moore: ''Moore, on the other hand, kept his head under his long fair locks, sideburns and mustachio that spoke of flower power and a psychedelic. Certainly it was he who gave the heartstrings a wrench of all the young female interflora on the sidelines. It was he who produced the squeaks of joy. And it was this energetic mind of his and an ability to change his tactics that pulled him through the final set when service was broken five times in seven games to leave the match in disorder."

The British seem so detached and serene to us that their true feelings often go unnoticed. In the days of austerity after the Second World War, when it seemed that economic recovery would never be achieved, nothing lifted British spirits as much as Randolph Turpin winning the middleweight championship from Sugar Ray Robinson. It was understandable in the circumstances, but for years now the national mood has been set for weeks at a time by the success or failure of Britain's footballers in the World Cup, and you can actually hear such an exchange as this:

INTERVIEWER: Could England fail to qualify for the World Cup?

EXPERT: It is treason to talk of England failing to qualify for the World Cup.

At the Olympics, the yearning for a British victory mingles with the remnants of a colonialist attitude, so that a French high jumper may be described as "a dark-skinned little man," or a Kenyan is said, patronizingly, to have "dignity on the track and in conversation," and there are references to "Japs," "great white hopes," and "the blacks who run for America."

In its purest form, British chauvinism expresses itself in a desire for Britain to win something. Anything. Thus the 10,000 meters in the 1972 Olympics, with the British commentator screaming about the British runner David Bedford, "The eyes of the world are on this man!" and the statement in the early stages, "The whole field, one suspects, is waiting for Bedford to make his move." When the race was over and Bedford, having had an off day, had come in twelfth, the commentator said, "Hmm. That was a curious run by Bedford. He never really made a positive move."

Pickings were so thin for the British in 1972 that a BBC commentator, otherwise bereft, spoke of one of the marathon runners this way: "Though he was born in Barrow-in-Furness, he is running for Australia, to which he emigrated. But if he does well, he'll give us some reflected glory."

Came the last day and one of the riding events, in which the British rider, Ann Moore, after doing poorly at the early fences, improved markedly. The commentator was beside himself: "Look at that — a great comeback by Ann Moore. That is what the Olympics are all about!"

This is reminiscent of a bit of folklorish nonsense in which the British sometimes indulge, when they say of an athlete that he is a Yorkshireman, i.e., dour, and therefore doesn't like to lose. We are left to believe that to athletes from other counties, not so dour, defeat is less unwelcome.

Inevitably, it is cricket that reveals the British at their most characteristic, for the game itself gives us the myths and legends and usages made concrete — the calm, the understatement, the greenness, the rules and rituals that in a larger context make it possible for so many people to live so close together without habitual mayhem and murder, and, fianlly, the clear understanding of what is "not cricket."

In British football, which we call soccer, a player kicking the skin or flesh off the legs of an opponent, or otherwise assaulting him, or using foul language to the referee, will "have his name taken." That carries an implicit threat of expulsion if the offense is repeated. In cricket it is not necessary to go that far. If a bowler is delivering the ball in such a way that it might well maim the batsman if it hit him, the umpire will "have a word with him."

Cricket also reveals the British sports writers at their most British. The cricket correspondent of the *Times* wrote not long ago that he had seen very poor performances by some players. "I will not name names this time," he added, "but if it should unfortunately become necessary, next time I will." Someone else's play, he wrote on another occasion when he did name names, "should be spoken of only in whispers."

One day in the summer of 1973 a BBC commentator remarked that a batsman had made an "abysmal" stroke. One of his colleagues became uncomfortable about it, and a discussion ensued over whether abysmal was justified. Eventually it was withdrawn and replaced by "indifferent," and no questions were asked in Parliament.

Indifferent is a useful word. It may be applied to what batsmen do, what bowlers do, and what fielders do. It strikes a suitably restrained note, providing condemnation without contumely, just as the crowd will often find the appropriate reaction to what is happening on the field in "a ripple of applause." There are some powerful hitters in cricket and some fiercely aggressive fast bowlers, but Britain is a moderate, temperate country in which a man captured by the police and about to be charged with the most appalling crimes is officially stated to be "helping the police with their inquiries." Cricket is a game to match. You rarely hear of a bowler helped by a strong wind. It is more seemly for him to have — and much more likely that he will have — "a slight breeze at his back."

In any case, superlatives are usually reserved for the weather. A glorious day is a day on which there is no downpour or steady drizzle.* A great day's cricket is a day on which the cricket has been exciting. This is not an easy thing to explain. A captain's innings (the captain is the playing manager) may not sound like a superlative but is meant to be,

* Fog may also be a problem, and is a greater one in football, which is played in the winter. During the football season you used to be able to count on seeing photographs of goalies peering anxiously out from the goal mouth, trying to make out what was happening downfield in the fog. The British have been cleaning their air, and these photographs are no longer so common.

describing a situation in which a team's batsmen have failed to make runs and the captain, when his turn comes in the order, scores well and saves the day. This may also be known as a real captain's innings. If the captain comes in and does poorly, it is not known as a captain's innings. This also is not an easy thing to explain.

I said earlier that cricket shows the British, and British sports writers, at their most characteristic. When cricket spread to Australia the attitude went with it. The following are excerpts from a column written by an Australian cricket correspondent after the Australian team's tour of Britain in 1972:

"As an old cricketer, I am a bit of a fogey when it comes to the privacy of dressing rooms, which belong exclusively to the players, and I have purposely not stayed at the same hotels as the Australians. If the players on a tour as long as this want to let their hair down occasionally, they are entitled to do so in privacy and it would be more than odd if fit-to-busting young athletes did not want to go on the rampage occasionally with a few drinks and songs.

"Cricketers of any country are not parlour saints. The Australians did not emerge with flying colors from Scotland and Northampton. They were careless in their approach to both games and at Northants apparently offended the shop steward of the waitresses by helping themselves to cheese and biscuits.

"Manager Ray Steel, a splendid manager with discipline but no stuffiness, dressed them down in no uncertain terms over their playing approach. He did not mention the cheese and biscuits.

"My hackles rise when I think they are criticized unfairly and it often strikes me as odd how the bare one or two, who were possibly no plaster saints on the field themselves, are so eager to dip their pens in vitriol against Australians. You would think we are not of the same stock.

"Once again, I say I am proud of these young Australians, even if they do not ask for the biscuits and cheese to be passed."

But as I learned early from W. Barrington Dalby, British sports writers do go in for colorful writing of the more familiar kind. When Muhammad Ali fought the British heavyweight Brian London in August, 1966, London was so inept that he aroused speculation about how he filled in his income tax form when he came to the blank for "occupation." The writers did considerably better than London, however. Some of them attributed the outcome to Ali's "killer punch," never seen before and not seen since, and the *Sunday Mirror* man gave forth this: "The 32-year-old bulldog was a dumbfounded spaniel at the finish."

There was no doubt that the thirty-two-year-old bulldog was knocked down, or at any rate had lost his balance. Most of the American writers at ringside preferred to be charitable and let slide the question of whether he could have continued. The British saw it in sterner terms. One had London "pawing impotently at the bottom rope like a man who had taken an overdose of sleeping pills." Another had him lying on his back, glassy-eyed. Still another wrote that London had been battered unconscious. One paper, a Socialist organ that earlier had been backward enough to refer to London as a white hope, used the headline, "London Is Blitzed!" Understandably, none went so far as to resuscitate "London Can Take It."

In the Ali-London fight, of course, the writers wanted to believe that Ali was an irresistible, even superhuman force. It helped the story. In other circumstances they react with less emotion and merely sigh and admit their mistakes. Thus the boxing correspondent of the *Times* of London on September 27, 1972: "I have never wished more deeply that I could have made a wrong prediction to the result of a boxing contest than last night at the Empire Pool, Wembley, when Bob Foster of the United States retained his world light-heavyweight title by knocking out Britain's champion, Chris Finnegan, after 55 seconds of the 14th round."

That was the sign. Now the admission:

"I had just said confidently to a steward of the British Boxing Board of Control, I don't believe in Foster's right, when the American promptly struck home with a right and Finnegan was down on his back, carefully taking a count of eight, after looking for instructions from his corner before he arose."

This is candid enough, but I am not certain that the *Times* boxing correspondent is entirely trustworthy. He once wrote, after an unsatisfactory bout, that he had heard "cries from ringside spectators of 'rubbish' and 'now bring on the phantom raspberry blower.'" "Rubbish," yes, but "bring on the phantom raspberry blower"? Even in a nation of eccentrics, that defies acceptance.

British boxing writers probably deserve sympathy more than scorn. Historically, especially among the heavyweights, they have had to make do with very little. That is why every time Muhammed Ali fights they report that he was once knocked down by Henry Cooper, the former British champion. That is why, when Ali fought Jerry Quarry for the second time, the British announced describing the fight for the BBC said almost disbelievingly that Ali was "toying with Quarry, toying with the man who knocked out Jack Bodell!"

Jack Bodell had become British heavyweight champion two months before meeting Quarry in November, 1971, and was dispatched by Quarry in 1:14 of the first round, and then a month later by Manuel Urtain of Spain in 1:41 of the second round, after which he lost to Danny McAlinden of Great Britain, after which he retired.

Jack Bodell! The mind boggles.

Britain today is a very different country from what it was when I saw it for the first time in 1949. And yet — and yet —

"When Liverpool, the favourites, and Newcastle United, the unpredictable, meet at Wembley this afternoon they could fashion a Cup Final of raw endeavour and spirit. It might be elemental: lightning on the field and thunder rolling down the terraces from the dwellers of Merseyside and Tyneside as two great clubs and two deep rivers join headlong in open challenge.

"Emotion rather than any rich vein of skill may dominate the occasion, with victory in the end claimed by patience and the steadier nerves. A year ago the

344

stadium shifted dramatically on its axis as Sunderland overcame all the odds to take the prize north-east at the expense of the powerful Leeds United.''

That is from the *Times* of London, May 7, 1974.

The terraces down which thunder rolls are parts of all British football stadiums, areas where the admission price is low and there are no seats: everybody stands. Some of those on the terraces are rowdy to the point of violence, and in a game in Manchester in April, 1974, thousands of them burst out onto the field and caused the match to be cut short. I heard a soccer correspondent explain that this kind of behavior was not peculiar to big cities like Manchester. It was, he said, the same in Weymouth, mutatis mutandis.

Mutatis and mutandis are bosom companions of those with classical educations; so long as British sports writers use them, we will know that Britain's literary tradition abides. When the sports writers say mutatis mutandiswise, we will know that the past is dead.

7

Soup as What the Chef Made

I have a small reputation as a gourmet. It is undeserved, as will appear, but at a time of a boom in cookbooks it has led to my receiving a fair number of requests for my favorite recipe, if possible accompanied by an anecdote. The requests come from people who say they are putting together books of recipes by celebrities that are guaranteed not to bring on gangrene or the pip, and who would like to have one from me.

The reputation led on one occasion to my being invited to address a luncheon at which awards were being given for the outstanding cookbooks of the year. I don't remember which books won, but among the entries that remained in the memory were *Mazel Tov Y'all,* a peculiarly graceful mingling of languages that sounded like the salutation of a southern politician seeking votes in the Catskills, and *The Pedernales Country Cookbook,* a book conceived of before President Johnson decided he would not run again but published afterward, by which time it had hardly more appeal than a study of the musical tastes of Calvin Coolidge. There was also *The "I Married an Italian" Cookbook,* by Bette Scaloni, who must have been terribly chagrined when she realized what she had done. I hope that at least it was hard cover and profusely illustrated.

So far as my qualifications as a cook go, I, like a lot of other men, lean to complicated recipes. Our cookery is based on the theory that the more ingredients a dish has, the better it is likely to be, so that any dish with sour cream, wine, the outer leaves of a head of lettuce, lemon juice, onion juice (what a job that is!), green pepper, monosodium glutamate, flour, curry powder, and dry mustard added to almost anything must have a stirring effect on those who eat it. The longer it takes, the better. Recipes that call for cooking over a period of days — "Allow the stew to simmer on top of the stove for 48 hours, stirring frequently" — are ideal. All this is still more the case if you use a lot of herbs. Men have faith in herbs. When I see them floating at the top of the pot, or flecking a chop, I know that success will soon be mine. Men also tend to make a lot of spaghetti, more than anybody can eat, especially at the beginning of their cooking careers.

I had two friends in college who were too poor for spaghetti and who made a dish using barley. They had no idea how much to cook and wound up depositing the surplus in brown paper bags on the doorsteps of people they didn't like.

But about the requests for recipes: I obliged only once, with a recipe for steak topped with a latticework of anchovies hugging — that's a cookery word, hugging — slices of olives stuffed with pimientos, and herb butter made with three herbs for the necessary excess. Magnifique! I wish I could remember its name. The other requests I declined because the reputation was cheaply won. It came about when I found myself living in Britain during the period of austerity after the Second World War, when greengrocers put out signs saying "Plums for All" and newspapers ran scare headlines like "Threat to Your Christmas Fruit and Nuts." Those were days when anybody whose gastronomic horizons went beyond cabbage, brussels sprouts, and cod was called a gourmet.

Not that I regret that time. It was rich in experience. I remember asking the flavor of the ice cream listed on the menu and being told, "Why, no flavor, sir," which turned out to be correct. And the waitress who, when asked for oil to put on hors d'oeuvres, replied, "The only oil we have at the moment, sir, is the oil we cook the chips in, and it's already been used, so it wouldn't be good." Or the waiter who, recommending rice pilaf, generously explained, "It isn't an English dish, sir, but it is very good." Or the waiter on the train between London and Penzance who, when asked what kind of soup was available, did not say, as tradition required, either that it was thick or that it was thin. He replied instead, "Soup as what the chef made."

Things were pretty bad in those days, as you will appreciate from the fact that newspapers printed recipes for carrot and turnip pie and a dish called fadge, which I will not go into further, and from the fact that a line of frozen food was sold under the catchy name "Frood." This naturally had its effect on the confidence of the British, and even the food advertisements sounded intimidated. I remember a green pea boasting that it was "first choice for second vegetable."

It has changed greatly now, of course. London is a good place for food and drink, and has been for years. This has much to do with the foreign influence. (I don't mean that Britain is entirely transformed. My daughter went into an English restaurant not long ago, and she and her companion asked whether they might have some wine. The proprietor looked at them with annoyance. "We don't do ween and all that tackle," he said.) It might be added also that the British unduly handicap themselves with the names they apply to some foods — bloaters, pilchards, scrag end, bubble-and-squeak, toad-in-the-hole, nosh, fry-up, faggots, roly-poly pudding, stodge, black pudding, spotted dog. These things would not be acceptable even if decked out in slavering American menu prose. I inserted three of them in a TWA menu encountered on a transatlantic flight:

BRAISED SCRAG END BOURGEOISE

A classic dish. The scrag end is slowly simmered in a rich stock of natural juices accentuated by a bouquet of fines herbes, small onions, and spices. Served with Château Potatoes and honey-glazed carrots.

GRILLED STODGE CUMBERLAND

From the broiler we present a generous portion of succulent stodge topped with Hawaiian pineapple ring and sprinkles of orange rind. Enhanced with a tangy red currant Cumberland

Sauce and accompanied by Duchess
Potatoes and a fluffy Broccoli Soufflé.

BLOATER SAINT HUBERT

This French creation was a favorite
of Saint Hubert, Patron of the Hunters.
In preparing this dish, tender young
bloater is cooked slowly in a zesty
tomato sauce with white wine, shallots,
and mushrooms. We serve it with
Parslied Potatoes and Mixed
Vegetables.

We have foreign influence in the United
States, too, as may be seen from the free
use of the word gourmet, which the
dictionary defines as a connoisseur in
eating and drinking, an epicure. A noun, in
other words, which is used more
frequently, in the United States, as an
adjective. For example, foods that used to
be known as delicacies, and which you
would get at the delicatessen or fancy
grocery, are now known as gourmet
foods, and you get them at a gourmet
store. Recently I saw a package of
gourmet blintzes. I don't think that the

blintz sees itself in that way. Maybe it could team up with knish lorraine. The two of them might go on the menu of an Israeli hotel in Jerusalem where gefilte fish came out carpe farçie traditionelle.

This use of the word gourmet is part of the increasing popularity of foreign words and phrases that are imperfectly understood, and you never know what you are going to run into when you enter a restaurant these days. I have come upon "restauranteurs" serving such exotic items as chicken soup a la raine; eminced chicken tetrazzini; lobster frad dabolo; o'grattan potatoes — made, one supposes, from an old Irish recipe; filet de mignon, perhaps from the opera by Ambroise Thomas; broiled filet of sole armandine, served, I imagine, with thin slices of the nut called the armand; bristling sardines, which may have been angry at being packed in that way; and for dessert, cake du jour. Some Americans think you can turn English words to French by adding an e, so that you have caramel custarde, and fruite, but cake needs stronger measures.

Similar to cake du jour in the way it weds two languages is the dish "eggs andalouse." A French restaurant on Forty-eighth Street in New York went that one better. It came out with eggs andalouise. I thought about this for a long time and concluded that the chef spoke with an Italian accent. One day a restaurant, or gourmet, correspondent asked him for the secret of this marvelous dish, and he replied that he got it from his Aunta Louise.

At another restaurant I was offered salaud de tomates, canapé d'anchovies, and egg in gélée, and invited to choose wine from a charto de vino. It reminded me of the liquor store in New York that proclaimed that it was selling wine of a fabulose vintage. And the place that called itself a saloon de thé.

A French restaurant in New York, or at any rate a restaurant with a French name, posts a menu du dinner. Quite by chance, it is not far from L'Embassy Coiffure and a drugstore that lists among the perfumes it sells Rêve Gauche.

The Loggia of the Polo Lounge of the

Beverly Hills Hotel in Los Angeles mentions coffee, tea, and milk under breuvages, which is ancient French and possibly survives only in Beverly Hills (Les Collines Beverly). But the Loggia comes unstuck over coconut with a cocoanut milk mousse, and serves lucious apple slices with its Dutch apple pancake.

A restaurant on the roof of a Los Angeles office building offers Chef's Specials du Jour, and another establishment lists Beef French Dip, thoughtfully giving us the recipe: "Choice thin sliced beef, dipped in au jus. Set on a French roll." And wheeled in on an a la carte.

Another New York restaurant says it has "a complete salad and antipasto table, where you can help yourself to as much as you'd like as a compliment to your meal." The night I was there I helped myself to only a little, because there was some question about whether my meal deserved a compliment, but I did send my supplements to the chef.

Language is so misused, English as well as foreign tongues, that I sometimes think of asking for my steak media rare. Perhaps those of us who are troubled by these developments would be better off staying at home. We would miss the complementary hors d'oeuvres but we could, after all, avoid menu misspellings by having our egg's benedict and bar-baqued chicken at home.

My job does not permit this. It calls for much travel. That is how it came about that a visit to Lincoln, Nebraska, produced a restaurant that offered Maderia wine and quoted Louis Pasteur to the effect that wine was the most healthful and hygenic of beverages. Not surprisingly the restaurant served, if it said so itself, Food Supérbo. Said food defied pronunciation, if not eating. Another establishment, a block away, listed on its menu the Italianoburger, which was a hamburger on an English muffin with mozzarella cheese and pizza sauce. Why was the English muffin left out of the title?

As long as I'm complaining — and my friends say that as long as I am awake I am complaining, which isn't true because in November, 1963, I covered the first annual International Banana Festival in Fulton, Kentucky, banana rail-transshipment capital of the United States, and saw a one-ton banana pudding being made, in a plexiglass container, of bananas, custard, and ginger snaps, and did not say an untoward word — as long as I'm complaining, I will go on with my theory about how 98 percent of the members of the waiters' union became waiters. It was because they couldn't remember the jobs they originally wanted to get.

I say this in memory of the old, passé assumption that waiters in a restaurant would remember what the customers ordered. Waiters whose memories were unreliable wrote down the orders and did it in such a way that they connected the items in question with those who asked for them.

No more. The art of waiting has undergone a transformation, and its language has shrunk almost to nothing. If a waiter is new to this country, there is little for him to learn. He is taught to say,

"Who gets the?" and then the names of the items on the menu after, or, if you prefer, subsequent to, "Who gets the?" With that, he is qualified. Not long ago I was in a group of five in a well-known New York restaurant. One person in the group ordered dessert, only one, and there was conversation between this person and the waiter about what it was to be. Nobody else took part in the conversation. One minute and forty-five seconds later the waiter reappeared with the single dessert. "Who," he asked triumphantly, "gets the sherbet?"

I cannot say with assurance that American restaurant food would be better if the spelling on menus were better or the waiters more conversant with their calling. But it would give diners more confidence, it would lend novelty to restaurant-going, and it *might* improve the cooking.

I have never been invited to address a luncheon at which awards were being given for the outstanding sex manuals of the year, but the language is much the same. Sex manuals are described as gourmet guides to lovemaking; as with cookbooks, consumer satisfaction depends on following the instructions implicitly; and if *The Joy of Cooking* tells you how to be happy at mealtime, *The Joy of Sex* offers between-meals snacks. Sex books are now as explicit and detailed as cookbooks, and have photographs intended to lead to coition as surely as photographs of Enchaud de Porc à la Périgourdine and Daube de Veau à l'Estragon are intended to encourage gluttony.

A bedroom is now to be thought of as a sindrome. In these days of sophisticated contraception it need not be in a condominium, but it is not complete without an illuminated stand next to the bed. The sex manual is placed on the stand so that the instructions may be followed as the lovemakers work their way through the foreword, chapters, footnotes, appendices, and index.

Ingredients:
Man (according to taste)
Woman (according to taste)

Bed, king-sized if possible

Mirror on ceiling, and also on wall

Incense

Flying trapeze

Whip

Champagne and four-course meal to be served during intermission

Artillery fire and pealing of Moscow church bells in Tchaikowsky's *1812 Overture*, cued to play at moment of climax

Tape recorder in form of phallic symbol into which participants may dictate their impressions as act proceeds.

Sexual fulfillment is becoming as compulsory as the gustatory kind. Civilization demands it, though in dining, if not in sex, the pleasure promised by the language employed exceeds any that is realized in fact. This is also true of travel. It may be especially true of travel:

"There's nothing ordinary in it because there's nothing ordinary about India. The dark eyes of gracious people. The highest mountains in the world. 5000 years of history in art and architecture. Temples. A tomb dedicated to love. Places and things out of the ordinary because they're in India."

"This season, why go south again? Head east. To the Soviet Union. Warm. Friendly. Hospitable. Come and celebrate the gala holiday season with us."

". . . the impeccable service of all-Italian personnel dedicated to your well-being and comfort, uncompromising quality and attention to detail. With it all, a spirited atmosphere that only a zestful Italian flair can achieve."

"Once, just once in your life. A long ocean cruise with Holland America. We think you deserve it. So we give you everything the unforgettable is made of."

"Give that cold, shivering body of yours a break. Escape the wrath of winter and come to a warm tropical island. To a delightful Holiday Inn resort, where all the comfort, conveniences, activities and fun-facilities are ready for your sun-drenched island adventure."

"This is not a tourist's cruise, bound for the long-exploited, over-exposed harbors.

This is an explorer's voyage through little-traveled waters into unfamiliar ports — each one affording a new, exotic experience. Vividly contrasting with the super civilized life aboard the *Renaissance,* so French in its cuisine, its solicitous French service, its gaiety aboard ship, its continuous round of diversions above and below decks."

"Elegant dining, elegant night clubs, elegant beaches, elegant opera, elegant ballet, elegant race track. Elegant people — the in-people, the beautiful people. This cornucopia of elegance is spilling out to all who take advantage of VIASA'S incredible $220 minimum to Caracas — to the city in the country in the Caribbean. To the most exciting tropical resort that's always been there but is only now being discovered."

"Meet the spirited, hospitable people in Golden PRAGUE. Wander through medieval settings beating with the pulse of modern life. Listen to the music of Anton Dvorak in his native land and stroll the footsteps of Franz Kafka through the cobblestoned streets of Josefov. Wine and dine in romantic BRATISLAVA on the blue Danube . . .''

It has long seemed to this cold and shivering body, dark-eyed, gracious, spirited, zestful, elegant, spirited and sun-drenched though it is, that tourism, even on cruises that are not tourist's cruises and are not bound for long-exploited, over-exposed harbors, is out of hand. Every spring and summer, all over the civilized world — which is to say those countries that are obliged to advertise themselves as tourist paradises because their own citizens can't bear them and insist on going abroad as soon as vacation time arrives — every spring and summer, millions of people prepare for the experience of a lifetime. The French go to Spain, the Spaniards go to France, the British go to Italy, the Italians to Britain, others cavort in Kafka's footsteps to the tune of a Slavonic dance; there is a vast amount of churning around, and there is enormous competition for going somewhere nobody you know has been. The way tourism is expanding, people will soon by paying for the privilege of a hike along the natural gas pipelines in the Algerian desert, or for exposing themselves to tropical diseases in the Matto Grosso.

The director-general of the Vatican museums recently wrote to the *Times* of London:

"We have installed 21 television cameras with centralized monitors to keep the traffic situation under control (we shall have 35 in a short time). We are using 18 'walkie-talkies' and highly trained attendants manning them, for securing prompt communications. Five spacious galleries have been equipped to keep visitors at a stand-by position until difficult situations clear up in front of them. A complete public address system is being installed to keep visitors informed and interested in the surroundings, with messages in five languages, while they have to wait. A busy control room is operating to secure the safe flow of our visitors and to decide exactly when and where it has to be slowed down or stopped and resumed."

It seems to me that this is a lot of

trouble, and expensive, and for the tourist nations self-defeating, and that there should be some easier way to do it.

Luckily, such a way lies to hand. It is an invention called the travel simulator. Everybody knows about those training devices the airplane pilot gets into and which lead him to believe that he is flying when he has never left the ground. The travel simulator operates on the same principle.

The travel simulator is an area, preferably at an airport, so that tourists are not deprived of the actual pleasure of going *there*. It could also be at a town terminal or at a specially equipped center financed by travel agencies, airlines, luggage manufacturers, hotel chains, and others dependent on tourist revenue. Wherever it is, the tourist must first call the airline on which he is booked to inquire about the flight departure, and be thanked for calling that airline, as though, having booked on TWA, he would be calling Northwest.

As the tourist enters the simulation area, he is given a check list on which he indicates the travel experiences he would like to have. Late departure of plane? There is a waiting room where he can sit, which is overheated and where the background music cannot be turned off. Flight overbooked? Tourist bumped? That can be arranged, and he can stay in the waiting room that much longer. If a sea voyage is preferred, it is a short step from motel beds that give you a mild shaking ("restful massage") for a quarter to a bed that can simulate rough seas and malfunctioning stabilizers. The seagoing passenger may, of course, choose the equivalent of the airliner passenger's overbooked flight — a strike in port.

Those who enjoy having their luggage lost have only to ask. Then, after checking into the hotel in the simulation area, they have no clothes to change into. That is, if they do check into the hotel. The clerks may have no record of the booking, and no rooms even if they do.

There are restaurants in the area. Tourists who like them overpriced, with uncooperative waiters, where Americans are made to feel unwelcome, have only to mark their forms accordingly. Women traveling alone can be turned away or, grudgingly, seated by the swinging kitchen door. No extra charge.

Hotels in the simulation area are either unfinished or getting a new wing, with construction work beginning outside your window at seven in the morning. Travel fatigue can be induced, as can digestive trouble — the makers of Entero-Vioforme may well be willing to underwrite the cost of this — and difficulty with the customs can be arranged when you return. ("Just think! You can be searched for dope!") Thanks to the magic of multi-media presentations, tourists can be taken on all-day jaunts of which the high point is an hour-long visit to a glass-blowing factory, where it is quickly made clear that you are grinding the faces of the poor if you do not buy. That is in the morning. In the afternoon there is a visit to a perfume factory, where those who do not buy are quickly marked out as wanting to bring on the poverty and resentment from which flow crime, war, and revolution. Unpleasant travel companions, specially trained and always on call, are thrown in as part of the basic package, as are fluctuating and unfavorable rates of exchange. A devaluation of the dollar and refusal to accept dollar traveler's checks — it's only fair — are counted as an optional extra.

In brief, the travel simulator gives the tourist all the thrills of travel without his ever leaving the airport. It does, nonetheless, take time, and in view of the demand for the service that is likely to arise, there are plans to provide a short course. In this the whole business would be telescoped, and tourists would be able to buy slides and journals of MY TRIP attesting to typical but exotic experiences according to the kind of conversation they want to have when they get home ("Really mind-stretching," "Wild," "What a gyp," "Was I ever glad to get home," "We had a ball," "There was this very nice hotel," "They told me to take my winter coat but I didn't need it," "I just went crazy," "The waiters came out with this very big tray," "We had seen that before," "I just have gone crazy here for a week," "I don't know how they live the way prices are there"). These and many more they could claim as their own, thus leaving them at no conversational disadvantage against those who have had the real thing, i.e., the full simulated trip.

Veterans in the field will be eager to supply such accounts for an appropriate fee. For example, in November, 1973, I spent a few days in Moscow. The door of my hotel room opened onto a flight of four steps, the top one of which had its center part gouged out; it was ideal for provoking a fall. The door opened inward, so that when you wanted to open it from the inside you had to climb the four steps, and then, as you opened the door, go back down. Just inside the door there was a light for a dressing alcove. To light the alcove it was necessary to climb the steps, then come back. The light was turned off the same way, of course. The alcove held two wooden cupboards for clothes. The drawers in the cupboards could not be used because the cupboard doors could not be opened because there was not enough room in the alcove.

Properly embellished, an account of all this, punctuated by nearly uncontrolled laughter and expressions of disbelief, can go on almost indefinitely.

If shorter reminiscences of simpler discomforts are needed, there was the time in Warsaw that I cut and bruised my knee on the footboard of the bed while getting up from the desk (I fall to the floor, holding my sides, while telling this one), and the bed in Jerusalem that seemed to be made of locally quarried stone. The essential point about such reminiscences is that they should have no intrinsic interest. All the foregoing qualify.

The idea of the travel simulator was born when I happened to find in Rome a leaflet the United States Travel Service had put out. The leaflet said: "Discover a new world of gastronomy. Visit the United States." It said that it was not true that Americans lived on coffee for breakfast, martinis for lunch, and frozen foods for dinner. It also explained that while the pioneers had had to use what they could find and borrow dishes from the Indians, these concoctions had since been refined. Being an American leaflet, it naturally misspelled the Caesar in Caesar salad. But no matter.

The Travel Service identified eight cooking regions in the United States. They were Gli stati dell' Atlantico Centrale, the Middle Atlantic States; Il Centro Ovest, the Middle West; Il New England; La regione dei creoli, that being Louisiana; Le Hawaii; La Pennsylvania Dutch; Il Sud, the South; and L'Alaska. The Italians were also told about drug stores. They were told that drug stores had developed so that their original function of selling medicines had become secondary, and that it was possible to take meals in them in an ambience without pretense (un ambienta senza pretese), which was a gentle way of putting it.

I soon had a vision of a tourist going to I Stati Uniti; and specifically to Gli stati dell' Atlantico Centrale, and to its greatest city, New York. Suppose that he had resigned himself to having gallons of ice water and ice cream forced down his throat, while legions of strangers told him their life stories and gave him their philosophies, and to being clubbed on general principles by any member of New York's finest who happened to catch sight of him, and that in search of a gastronomic discovery he took a city bus as transport to a native eatery. New York City buses have signs in them asking for contributions to the Legal Aid Society, the Visiting Nurses Service, the Greater New York Fund, the Boys Clubs of America, the Catholic Youth Organization, the Young Men's Christian Association, the Federation of Jewish Charities — and also give to the college of your choice. A visitor might get the impression that we are in pretty awful shape if he rode a charity bus. But suppose he took an illness bus, the kind in which the signs ask for help to fight cancer, heart disease, multiple sclerosis, cerebral palsy, hemophilia, tuberculosis, mental retardation, and mental illness, among others. Afraid? Sick? Lonely? one sign asks. Christian Science Can Help.

New York is a vast sanitarium. Some buses used to carry signs that said one

New Yorker in ten is mentally ill and needs help. Taken literally, from a pocket Italian-English dictionary, that could have been interpreted to mean that there is one chance in ten that your driver is a mental case. Now there is a new one: Rape Report Line. 233-3000. A policewoman will help you. The tourist's appetite for a scoperto gastronomico is not likely to survive this. Still another sign may well convince him that *he* will not survive:

> There's so much beauty in the blooming
>   Rose
> And through its life, Who knows where
>   it goes?
> Some Roses will live over a season
>   through
> While others will enjoy part of the dew.
>
> But even Roses with all their splendor
>   and heart
> Will one day their beautiful petals fall
>   apart.
> Man too, has his season like the Rose
> And then, one day, he also must repose.

The sign is placed by Unity Funeral Chapels, Inc., whose slogan is, We Understand.

The simulator is better.

8

The Vicious Cycle of Reality

There are millions of people who groan when they hear a pun. It is a standard response, and my impression is that they are simply envious or bent on denying themselves one of the delights that language offers.

I made no apology for punning. I have been at it for a long time, and a small, if anonymous, place in history belongs to me because of a pun. In December, 1945, I called a speech on Soviet-American relations by Secretary of State James F. Byrnes ''The Second Vandenberg Concerto'' because of its similarity to a speech made by Senator Arthur

Vandenberg a short time before. This is reproduced in Ambassador Charles Bohlen's book *Witness to History,* though without credit to me. At the time of its conception it was printed in a number of newspapers and magazines, attributed to "a press room wag." A good wag is hard to find.

Sometime in 1960 I put forward "Pompidou and Circumstance" to identify the conditions in which a French government might fall. *Time* used this before I could, presumably getting it from a wag of its own, and leaving me with no more chance of claiming it than someone would have trying to take credit for the incandescent lamp from Thomas A. Edison.

To repeat, I make no apology for punning, and specifically for what follows. I am proud of it.

"Where have you been?" she asked.

"Out walking the dog," he said. "Looking for the old familiar feces."

"Your shoes are wet," she observed.

"Naturally," he said. "Nobody knows the puddles I've seen. That is why I am standing on these newspapers. These are the *Times* that dry men's soles." He took off his jacket and tossed it aside. "This," he said, "is so sodden."

"I'll never forget the time they brought you in frozen stiff," she said. "I was afraid you'd never come out of it."

He shrugged. "I thawed, therefore I am."

"I believe that dog has distemper or worms or something," she said.

"Maybe so," he replied, "but his bark is worse than his blight. By the way, I'm thinking of giving him to the Longshoremen's Union as a mascot."

"What kind of dog do they want?"

"A dockshund."

"I'm lonely," she said, and pointed to a button she was wearing that bore the words "Kiss me. I'm Irish."

"I'm hungry," he said. "Quiche me. I'm French."

She gave him instead a pastry consisting of thin layers of puff paste interlaid with a cream filling. He cut off a corner and ate it.

"Very good," he said. "Also the first

square mille feuille I've had all day."

"Your French is getting better," she said. "I can remember when you thought the French for throw out the bag was cul-de-sac."

"O solecism mio," he said. "And I can remember when you thought a porte-cochere was the entrance to a Jewish restaurant."

There was a moment's pause. Then:

"I had an apprentice French hairdresser once," she said.

"What did he have to say for himself?"

"Je ne sais coif."

"Having a man around the house does make a vas deferens," she continued.

"And having a woman around, too," he said gallantly. "You're a wonderful housekeeper. You keep everything polished."

"Maybe so," she said, "but I wish I could chamois like my sister Kate. I meant to ask you, did you watch the space shot at the office?"

"No," he replied. "To me the space program is a mere schirrade. I decided to go to a movie instead, the one in which

378

Montgomery Clift plays the founder of psychoanalysis."

"What was his name again?"

"Pretty Boy Freud."

"I notice that in the early days of photography he had his picture taken with his coat on and looking furtive. Any idea why?"

"He must have been a cloak and daguerrotype."

She changed the subject. "I am glad we're out of Vietnam."

"So am I. It was time to let Saigon be Saigon's."

"What do you make of the situation between the Russians and Chinese?" she asked.

"Dogma eat dogma."

"You said a Maothful."

"Tell me, how was your trip to Washington?"

"All right," she said, "but the taxi driver insisted on talking. I felt that I was a cabtive audience."

"What was it you had to do there?"

"Deliver two messages."

"To whom?" he asked.

"One was to the junior Senator from Mississippi."

"Any trouble?"

"No. I was directed to a room where the Armed Services Committee was meeting, and I simply went in and asked, 'Stennis, anyone?' "

"What was the message, by the way?"

"Just what you'd wish any politician during the festive season: a Merry Charisma and a Happy New Year."

"And the other?" he asked.

"That was more difficult," she said. "The nonferrous metals industry was holding a meeting and I had to find the one ferrous metals man who was there. Luckily I was able to go into the ladies' room and say, 'Mirror, mirror, on the wall, who's the ferrous one of all?' "

"Any luck?" he asked.

"Oh, yes," she said.

"What did you do about lunch?" he wanted to know.

"I had Chinese," she said.

"Not Korean?"

"No, though I do like Seoul food."

"Was the Chinese any good?"

"Not really. I sent back the soup."

"Any reason?"

"I told the waiter it had been tried and found Won Ton."

"You've done better."

"When?"

"That cold day at the Four Seasons when you didn't like the cooking and you told the head waiter, 'Now is the winter of our discontent.' But what happened after you sent back the Won Ton?"

"They brought me some consomme."

"How was it?"

"Much better. It was a consommé devoutly to be wished."

"I'd like to have a Chinese meal in Alaska someday," he said musingly.

"Why is that?"

"I'd like to try lo mein on a totem pole."

She was lost in thought for a moment, then blushed lightly. "I don't think I've ever told you that I originally intended to marry a clergyman."

"Why didn't you?"

"Because," she said, humming softly, "I picked a layman in the garden of love when I found you."

It was his turn to hum.

"What are you humming?" she asked.

"The volcano's torch song," he said. "Lava, come back to me."

She pouted.

"This time of year seems to bring out the worst in you," he said.

"I know," she replied. "I'm often jejune in January."

"Sometimes I think you've never got over your regret at not being born a blonde."

"Not quite true. Actually, I dream of genealogy with the light brown hair. Wasn't it a shame about Father O'Reilly being mugged the other night after the ecumenical meeting?"

"He can't say he wasn't warned. Rabbi Goldstein was most explicit."

"What did he say?"

"Do not go, gentile, into that good night."

"And that didn't stop Father O'Reilly?"

"I'm afraid not. He left without further adieu."

"I thought that Father O'Reilly was

going to give up the Church. I thought he had decided he preferred law to religion.''

''Just the opposite. He said he'd rather be rite than precedent.''

''Do they know who did it?''

''No, but they do know that the muggers were young and were laughing as they left.''

''Jubilant delinquents?''

''Exactly.''

''If the case comes to court, will you be a witness?''

''No, though I may put in a friend of court brief.''

''That hardly seems necessary.''

''It isn't, but if I don't submit one, it may be said that I'm amicus curiae yellow.''

''And if they don't catch them?''

''Well, honi soit qui nolle prosse.''

''I have to tell you that we got word today that we are overdrawn.''

''Bankers Thrust.''

''In spite of which I intend to spend some money tonight to go to hear Gloria Steinem speak.''

''Women's Glib,'' he said. ''Tote that

barge, lift that veil. But isn't it your night for tennis?''

"My racket is being repaired. One of the strings broke.''

"A gut reaction.''

"I bought a book of British seafood recipes today.''

"May I guess at the title?''

"Please.''

"What Hath Cod Wrought?"

"No. It's *Cod et Mon Droit.*''

"By the way, the cod war between Britain and Iceland did end, did it not?''

"Yes, it was followed by the cod peace.''

"I spent some money, too,'' he said. "I got us ballet tickets for *Giselle.*''

"There *is* nothing like Adam.''

"I'm always embarrassed at the way people fidget when they play 'The Star-Spangled Banner' before the curtain goes up. We should have learned long ago that a short anthem turneth away wrath.''

"I'd rather go to a movie than the ballet.''

"Any one in particular?''

"Yes, that western with the Old

Testament background — *Armageddon for the Last Roundup.*"

"To go back to cookbooks, you do get some strange ones."

"What do you mean?"

"Well, there was *Kurds and Whey,* the only book ever put out by the Kurdish Publishing Company."

"I did get the publisher's name wrong."

"You've heard me mention my friend Bales, the chemist?"

"Yes."

"He's lost his job."

"Whatever for?"

"The company wanted him to work on acetates, and he refused."

"Because he who acetates is lost?"

"Precisely. Even worse, when he was asked to explain himself, all he would say was, 'I have no retort.' "

"Is he looking for another job?"

"He's thinking of going into advertising, but he's hesitating. He says he feels it would be crossing the Young and Rubicam."

A sweet voice came from the kitchen. "Would you like some tea, Daddy?"

"Yes, my darjeeling, daughter." He turned back. "She sounds so sad these days. You'd think a girl pretty enough to be a model would be happy."

"It's modeling that's done it. It's turning her into a manne-quin-depressive."

The sweet voice rose in anger. "It isn't. It's these hot, cross puns. Will you two never stop?"

They did.

So will I, in spite of having a reserve that includes Pilat project, buying cigars from the Good Humidor man, détente saving time, Gdansk, ballerina, Gdansk as advice to a Polish girl unable to make it with the Bolshoi, a worried Dutch conductor with the Concernedgebrow, a Middle Eastern psychiatrist known as the shrink of Araby, and a Japanese robot functioning shakily because of a recent frontal robotomy.

All the foregoing puns were invented. Of what follows, only the framework was invented. Everything else was seen or heard by me. Truth is stranger than fiction.

I hark back to a day when my wife and I went to a nuptual mass. We were not in the best possible mood for it because we were tired of the up-evils of daily life. Although we had not yet reached our autumn, or reclining, years, we wanted a cover for our chaise lounge but had not been able to arrange it. The delivery people never seemed to do enough pre-planning and were always flaunting the public.

I recommended to my wife that she calm her nerves by having her hair style changed at Mercede's Beauty Salon, which had done outstandingly well the day she had had her picture taken at the Select Photo Studio's. She followed my suggestion.

After the nuptual mass, we went to a café where the background music consisted of Tchaikovsky's "Variations on a Rococco Theme." There we met another couple and there also we fell to admiring the figure of a girl at the next table.

"It is possible," the other woman at our table said, "for the rest of us to have a figure like hers. Take up fencing. I have just bought a book of fencing instructions." She thereupon produced the book, called *En Guarde,* which proved to be an insightful essay on the value of the sport.

The meeting soon became one of those social engagements that drag on. Tchaikovsky's music gave way to a composition by Hector Burlio, culture was at fervor pitch, and when the male half of the other couple pulled out his imperial old bruyer pipe and began smoking, it was easy to see that we were in for a long session of badgering words back and forth.

After a while he put the pipe down, which I welcomed because I was feeling quasi, and told us about a friend who had carved out a notch for himself and reaped a veritable bonzana from investing in a company that restored richly designed Chinese objects d'art. Unfortunately, the bonzana was followed by a hollowcast because his friend took to drink and contracted multiple cirrhosis.

Our friend's wife was just back from

Europe. She told us how much she enjoyed eating spaghetti a la dente in Italy, sauerbratin in Germany, and vichysoir in Paris, where she also visited Napoleon's tomb in the Invalidays.

At this point, the waiter, who had perked up his ears, came over, but our friend, not hungry, merely ordered a Puerto Rican Libre, austensible successor to the Cuba Libre. We all ordered something to drink, and a man in the corner, possibly an Asian provocateur, came over and asked us to join in a toast to the unconquerable spirit of Britain, as revealed in Westminister Abbey. We did, and after saying that he believed that Britain soon would rise to new platitudes of achievement, the man retired.

The bruyer pipe smoker at our table, strongly patriotic, said it would be beggaring the question to deny that the American defense build-up, conventional and nucular, had given the western alliance new and powerful strength, and if he guaged things correctly, this was what Western Europe in the last resource relied on. He did not, of course, wish to appear chargined, but he thought that things had not been right since the days when Charles de Gaulle mistakenly thought of himself as another Joan D. Arc, intent on filling his countrymen with spirit de corps.

After that, there seemed to be no reason to go on with this fol de roy. My wife and I decided to escape from the vicious cycle of reality by going to a performance by the English ballet troop from Covent Gardens. I would have preferred the Comédie François but it was not in town, and anyway, we had received the ballet tickets as a free bonus gift.

We went and enjoyed it, possibly because we are homogenous types and have a good rappaport. Neither of us behaves aggressibly and if one wants to do something, the other is usually successible. As a result, we are evolving toward a better adjustment vis-à-vis our environment. You never know, of course, but at any rate, up to the present junction.

The publishers hope that this Large Print Book has brought you pleasurable reading. Each title is designed to make the text as easy to see as possible. If you wish a complete list of the Large Print Books we have published, ask at your local library or write directly to:

G. K. Hall & Co.
70 Lincoln St.
Boston, Mass. 02111